THE GREAT SHIFT

And How To Navigate It

Michael Drake

THE GREAT SHIFT

10-digit ISBN: 0-9629002-9-X
13-digit ISBN: 978-0-9629002-9-7
Talking Drum Publications
http://ShamanicDrumming.com

The shamanic methodology presented in this book should not be viewed as a substitute for orthodox medical or psychological treatment, but should instead be considered a complementary treatment. This book is not intended as a substitute for the medical advice of physicians. The reader should regularly consult a physician in matters relating to his/her health and particularly with respect to any symptoms that may require diagnosis or medical attention. I trust you will use your own discretion and intuitive wisdom as to how shamanic practice may be appropriate to your particular needs.

Printed in the United States of America

Cover image created by Reto Stockli with the help of Alan Nelson, under the leadership of Fritz Hasler at NASA Goddard Space Flight Center.

MICHAEL DRAKE

Dedication

To the Keepers of the Pipe

THE GREAT SHIFT

Contents

THE GREAT SHIFT

Acknowledgments

I would like to express my gratitude to:

My wife Elisia, whose love and support allowed me to bring this work to fruition. She has been my inspiration and motivation for writing this book;

Cathy Dawn Perkins for her guidance, insight and vision. She is a true hollow bone; a clear conduit between the spirit world and the human world;

Peggy and Luke Sayben for helping me write and edit the first appendix in this book. I am blessed to have your guidance, friendship and support;

My helping spirits, whose guidance gave this book much needed direction.

THE GREAT SHIFT

MICHAEL DRAKE

Introduction

The Great Shift is about the new era of humanity. As the Information Age evolves into the Shift Age, we are entering an epic time of change and transformation that offers both great challenge and unparalleled opportunity. Our present world is one in which order is arising out of chaos. Everything is changing and seeking equilibrium. The conditions are nothing short of a rebirth. We are entering uncharted waters, for the situation we face is unlike any that we have experienced before. We have entered the new epoch of humanity's evolutionary journey into higher consciousness.

This book is a guide to navigating the shift from an old paradigm into a new one. It is deeply rooted in the shamanic and Taoist (pronounced Daoist) traditions, which are a fountain of wisdom and knowledge for restoring our relationship with the Earth. Both traditions place great emphasis on personal experience derived from introspection and self-observation. Though they differ significantly in their approach, practitioners of both traditions seek accord with nature through consciousness-altering techniques. A brief introduction and overview of each tradition will facilitate your understanding of the ideas and concepts they embody.

Shamanism

Shamanism is the most ancient and most enduring spiritual tradition known to humanity. It predates and constitutes the foundation of all known religions, psychologies and philosophies. It originated among nomadic hunting and gathering societies. These ancient shamanic ways have withstood the tests of time, varying little from culture to culture. Over thousands of years of trial and error, primal peoples the world over developed the same basic principles and techniques of shamanic power and healing. A whole way of life evolved that was based on everything being in right relationship.

In the worldview of the shaman, all life forms are interconnected and interdependent. If one species suffers, all others are affected. The health and well-being of humanity is, therefore, dependent upon the overall health of the sentient web of life. The shaman is sensitive to this sacred interrelationship and serves as a bridge, linking the human and natural

9

realms. The shaman's prayerful communion with the natural elements and powers preserves an orderly, harmonious universe.

Christina Pratt, shamanic healer, teacher and author of *An Encyclopedia of Shamanism*, defines a shaman as a practitioner who has developed the mastery of "accessing altered states of consciousness" and "mediating between the needs of the spirit world and those of the physical world in a way that can be understood by the community ...."[1] Shamanism is the spiritual practice of ecstasy. Ecstasy is defined as a mystic, prophetic or poetic trance. Practitioners enter altered states of consciousness in order to perceive and interact with the inner world of the self. The act of entering an ecstatic trance state is called the soul flight or shamanic journey.

Rhythmic drumming is a simple and effective way to induce ecstatic trance states. When a drum is played at an even tempo of three to four beats per second for at least fifteen minutes, most people can journey successfully even on their first attempt. Transported by the driving beat of the drum; the practitioner journeys to the inner planes of consciousness to obtain personal revelation and spiritual experience.

According to shamanic cosmology, there are three inner planes of consciousness: the Upper, Middle, and Lower Worlds. The three realms are linked together by a vertical axis that is commonly referred to as the cosmic axis or World Tree. This central axis exists within each of us. Through the sound of the drum, which is invariably made of wood from the World Tree, the shaman is transported to the axis within and conveyed from plane to plane.

The shaman traverses the inner planes in order to change and shape experience. It is an inward spiritual journey of rapture in which the shaman interacts with the inner world, thereby influencing the outer world. In the shaman's world, all human experience is self-generated. Experience is shaped from within since the three realms or resonant fields that define our experience of reality exist within each of us.

The essence of shamanism is the experience of direct revelation from within. Shamanism is about remembering, exploring and developing the true self. Shamanism places emphasis on the individual, of breaking free and discovering one's own uniqueness in order to bring something new back to the community. Shamanic practice heightens the ability of perception and enables you to see into the deeper realms of the self. Once connected with your inner self, you can find help, healing, and a continual source of guidance. To practice shamanism is to reconnect with your deepest core values and your highest vision of who you are and why you are here.

Taoism

Taoism originated in China between 600 and 500 BC, but the roots of Taoism can be traced back to shamanic practices from the earliest tribal communities. The Chinese word for shaman (*wu*) was first recorded during the Shang Dynasty (1600-1046 BC), but it is believed that these traditions date back to the very origins of Chinese culture. In fact, many of the stories surrounding Fu Hsi (or Fu Xi), the mythological founder of Chinese civilization are very shamanic. For example, Fu Hsi is considered the originator of the I Ching, an ancient Chinese divination text and the basis of Chinese thought. According to legend, he discovered the symbols of the I Ching in the pattern of markings on the back of a turtle that emerged from a river. This is a classic shamanic tale that combines nature and divination, resulting in the attainment of profound knowledge.

Philosophical Taoism, often represented by the yin-yang symbol, emphasizes living in harmony with the Tao (the Way), or Ultimate Reality, a presence that existed before the universe was formed and which continues to guide the natural world and everything in it. Tao is the ultimate source and way (or process) of nature and the universe. To live in harmony with the Tao is to go with the flow of life rather than against it. It is a way to conserve life's vitality by not expending it in the useless ways of friction and conflict. Early Taoists perceived that the ultimate nature of this mysterious force was beyond intellectual comprehension but could be discerned by the intuitive mind. The sages observed that through meditation, one could attain Tao or communion with the way of the universe itself.

Through meditation and other devotional activities, Taoists seek to bring their lives into accord with the Tao. They believe that by abiding in the Tao, or in harmony with the Cosmos, one may attain a state of such inner clarity and insight that all actions become synchronous and spontaneously correct. They refer to this state of harmony with nature and the universe as *wu wei*, or "non-doing." Non-doing is not a withdrawal from action, but rather the achievement of a higher kind of action: action in accord with the natural order. The concept of *wu wei* more closely suggests a way of existing without conscious effort, as nature does. Such a person knows what to do by abiding in a state of quietism, by letting go of all worldly thought so that the creative force of the Tao may enter their minds and bodies. Such accord with the Tao allows one to accomplish things without effort in a way that benefits everyone.

Taoism is an inner way as well as an outward path. One should outwardly "go with the flow" while inwardly adhering to one's true nature. Taoists seek to integrate inner and outer experiences while uniting body, mind and spirit into a harmonious whole. Taoism views humanity as a microcosm of the macrocosm we call the universe. Each human being is a hologram of the Cosmos, a weaving together of universal information from a particular point of view. Essentially, we are the universe experiencing itself in human form.

Taoists equate the body with the earthly realm, the mind with the human realm, and the spirit with the heavenly realm. By bringing the body, mind and spirit into accord, one transforms personal experience and influences the interactions of the three cosmic realms. Following the Tao is a journey requiring simplicity, balance and introspection. The lifelong quest of the Taoist is to identify their innermost purpose in life, and then use every means at their disposal to achieve it.

Comparing traditions

Shamanism and Taoism are a way of living in harmony with nature, rather than an adherence to a religious doctrine. By practicing these ways of being, we awaken our soul calling and our connection to nature. Both traditions are ultimately about consciousness, about learning through attunement to nature. They provide a myriad of responses to the spiritual quest of self-discovery. Both paths emphasize establishing a personal relationship with the powers of creation. They are ways that embed us in the living web of life, yielding greater awareness and perspective. These practices are easily integrated into contemporary life and provide a means of navigating the turbulent times in which we live.

Both the shaman's and the Taoist's universe is three tiered. Both traditions maintain that there are three realms or resonant fields that define our experience of reality. The triad of heaven-earth-man is the self-existing order of the universe. Sustained by the Earth and transformed by the heavens, humanity is the bridge that unites the three realms. In harmonizing the microcosm of the self with the macrocosm of the universe, we harmonize heaven and Earth.

MICHAEL DRAKE

Chapter 1

The Great Shift

We have entered the Shift Age: the time of transition in the evolution of human consciousness from separateness to a planetary frame of reference.
—David Houle, American futurist and author of *This Spaceship Earth*[1]

We are living during extraordinary times. So very many are asking the same question these days: "What is happening around us?" We live in a time of accelerated change and transformation. We see severe climate change, massive oil spills and species dying off. We see corruption in banking, politics and religions around the world. We see fear, anger and hopelessness in our communities. Greed, poverty, violence and injustice are predominant characteristics of our civilization. What on earth is happening?

A growing number of voices in the international shamanic community are telling us that Mother Earth and her inhabitants are undergoing a fundamental, evolutionary change—a change that many of us will experience first-hand in this lifetime. Some call it the Kali Yuga, the age of maximum darkness and ignorance; a time when the dark forces of the unconscious are at their strongest. Some call it the Era of Strife, Tribulations, or End of Days. Others refer to this unfolding event as the Turning of the Age or a Great Shift in consciousness that was foretold long, long ago. This is an exciting time to be present on the Earth. It is a time filled with unparalleled opportunities for spiritual growth.

The cycle of time

The ancients understood time as circular rather than linear. In Chinese philosophy, yin and yang, the feminine and masculine aspects of the universe, vibrate and spiral in a sacred dance, giving birth to the sonic pulse of the Cosmos. Yin and yang ebb and flow; creating the cycle of time. Behind the cycle of time lies an ongoing evolution of consciousness. Just as a tree has annual cycles of growth and retreat but continues to grow year after year, so all things have an inner growth process in which consciousness continues to develop through life after life.

The civilization process goes through four eras or ages. Like the four seasons in our year, there are four stages to man's evolution in the full cycle. Each cycle has distinct themes and spiritual lessons for humanity. Ancient astrology places humanity under the legendary four ages: the Golden, Silver, Bronze and Iron ages. We find this belief in world ages among the Greeks as well as the Hindus. In Sanskrit, an ancient language of India, these are called the yugas or world ages of Satya (the first), Treta (the second), Dvapara (the third), and Kali (the fourth). After the world fall at the end of the fourth, worst age (the Kali Yuga), the cycle starts again.

Hindus believe that civilization degenerates spiritually during the Kali Yuga, which is referred to as the Dark Age because in it people have turned away from the light of truth and virtue. Hinduism often symbolically represents morality (*dharma*) as an Indian bull. In Satya Yuga, the first stage of development, the bull has four legs, but in each successive age morality is reduced by one quarter. By the age of Kali, morality is reduced to only a quarter of that of the Golden Age, so that the bull of Dharma has only one leg. In the Kali Yuga, time speeds up or, more precisely, *karma* speeds up. In Sanskrit, *karma* is the spiritual principle of cause and effect where intent and actions of an individual (cause) influence the future of that individual (effect). But the truth is, according to Vajrayana Buddhist teachings, this intensification makes this an exceptional time for spiritual practice, because the fruits of such practice are now more magnified and immediate. Even in the worst of times, the possibility to be well above it is always there for an individual human being. This is a time filled with unparalleled opportunities for spiritual growth and inner transformation.

The purpose of this Great Shift, we are told, is to establish a new era, a Golden Age of peace and harmony on the Earth plane so that humanity may experience love in ways it cannot yet comprehend. The current upheaval in society must occur. Destruction is a part of creation. We live in a world of endless cycles. We are quite literally witnesses and participants in the shift from an old paradigm into a new one. We are part of the emerging consciousness, and the signs are everywhere. It is here now, and we all have a part to play in it.

MICHAEL DRAKE

Shamanic wisdom for the Anthropocene age

Scientists have determined that we are now living in the Anthropocene age: the new epoch of geological time in which human activity is considered such a powerful influence on the environment, climate and ecology of the planet that it will leave its legacy for millennia. The Anthropocene is notable as being human-influenced, or anthropogenic, based on overwhelming global evidence that atmospheric, geologic, hydrologic, biospheric, and other Earth system processes are now altered by humans. In the Anthropocene, humans move from a biological to a geological agent. The Anthropocene is distinguished as a new period after or within the Holocene, the current epoch, which began approximately 10,000 years ago (about 8000 BC) with the end of the last glacial period.

Now that the age during which all human civilization developed is ending, it might be time to pay more attention to the experience of those whose world has already ended: indigenous peoples. Depending on how you count them, there may be up to three hundred million indigenous people still on the planet. Most are survivors of colonialism. The genocide of the Native Americans was the beginning of the modern world for Europeans, but the former remain as veritable end of the world experts. Models for restoring our relationship with the Earth exist in the cultures of indigenous peoples, whose values and skills have enabled them to survive centuries of invasion and exploitation.

Native American perspectivism

Establishing a relation to indigenous thought and practice is no simple task. Not only do we have different views, understandings, perceptions and cultures that see the world in different ways, we inhabit very different worlds. Native American conceptions are grounded in perspectivism: the philosophical view that there are many different world views depending on an individual's particular perspective. Put another way, every entity views every entity and event from an orientation peculiar to itself. Perspectivism holds that only one spirit exists in everything. It implies that everything is alive, sentient and shares a common spiritual essence.

Perspectivism assumes multinaturalism, which is the polar opposite of our multiculturalism. In multiculturalism, there is only one nature, but there can be many cultures, and it sets about studying, documenting and classifying them. By contrast, in multinaturalism, there is only one culture (spirit/soul) and multiple natures. From a Native American point of view, there is no singular nature as such because perception is dependent on perspectives (humans perceive nature differently than animals, and animals perceive nature differently than spirits, and so on), yet none of these natures is absolute and they are all just as valid.

Another way to view the difference is to put it like this: Westerners see themselves physically as animals and spiritually different; Native Americans see themselves spiritually as animals and physically different. Native Americans inhabit a radically different conceptual universe than ours where nature and culture, human and nonhuman, subject and object are conceived in terms that reverse our own. Every entity is conceived as having a soul—intentionality and conscious perception—like a human being. Moreover, all beings perceive themselves as humans and other beings as animals. While viewed by humans as animals, animals and other beings regard themselves (their own species) as human and live in conditions similar to humans; that is, they have a social and cultural life similar to those who inhabit a Native American village.

Establishing an authentic relationship with other beings therefore requires adopting their perspectives, as shamans do when they shapeshift into animals. Shamans will shapeshift into an animal so as to see the world through their eyes and to feel what they feel. Shamanism is a practice of defying the limits of human perspective, crossing borders into the social worlds of other species, administering relations between natures. Essentially, the shaman is a diplomat who creates a dialogue with other beings. As Brazilian anthropologist Eduardo Viveiros de Castro puts it, "By seeing nonhuman beings as they see themselves (again as humans), shamans become capable of playing the role of active interlocutors in the trans-specific dialogue and, even more importantly, of returning from their travels to recount them; something the 'laity' can only do with difficulty."[2]

The mythical paradise

To better understand Native American perspectivism, it is necessary to explore its mythological aspects. Native Americans were cosmocentric rather than ethnocentric. Native American myths take place at a time when the Cosmos' multiple entities shared a collective human condition and were thus able to communicate with each other. The mythology and

16

creation stories of all indigenous peoples speak of a primordial, but now lost paradise in which humanity lived in harmony with all that existed. The Cosmos had total access to itself. There was but one language for all creatures and elements. Humans were able to converse with animals, birds, minerals; all nature's creations.

While in the primeval times, all beings were perceived as human and nonhuman simultaneously, or in a state of constant transformation into one or another of these forms. Mythical animal characters were commonly portrayed as essentially human in physical form, but possessed the individual characteristics attributed to the various types of animals as they exist in nature today. Myths describe how, at some point, this generic human condition undergoes severe disruption, resulting in the transformation of the many types of humans that existed—already differentiated by the physical or behavioral characteristics of the nonhuman beings they would eventually become—into the different present-day species of animals, plants and other kinds of beings.

After the cosmic rupture, the shaman became essential as he could reconstitute the mythical paradise. In our day, as in times past, the shaman is able to access the mythic realm of reality through techniques of ecstasy. Shamanism is based on the principle that the social worlds of other species may be contacted through the inner senses in ecstatic trance induced by shamanic practices such as repetitive drumming. The drum provides the shaman a relatively easy means of controlled transcendence. Researchers have found that if a drum beat frequency of around three to four beats per second is sustained for at least fifteen minutes, it will induce significant trance states in most people, even on their first attempt.

The act of entering an ecstatic trance state is called the soul flight or shamanic journey, and it allows the journeyer to once again communicate with animals, plants and all living things. Shamans believe that this direct communication is possible because the entire universe exists within human consciousness. The capacity to enter a range of trance states is a natural manifestation of human consciousness. Our journeying ability is part of our human heritage. The ability to enter trance states makes us a human, not a shaman. What makes shamans unique is their mastery over an otherwise normal human trait. It requires training, practice and devotion to master any expressive art. Shamanic practitioners master the art of ecstasy to see the different realities of the universe.

The dismemberment journey

In shamanism, there is an archetypal visionary experience known as the dismemberment journey. The student or practitioner of shamanism recognizes an illusion or fear that impedes the expansion of their soul. The practitioner prays for this flaw to be healed and, in doing so, surrenders to the wisdom of the higher powers of the universe to remove the impediment. In a classic dismemberment journey, the petitioner witnesses their own body being torn apart and perhaps completely destroyed. The individual dies a symbolic death and is then restored and brought back to life, whole and empowered, the fear or illusion vanquished.

From an indigenous perspective, the Anthropocene represents a mass shamanic dismemberment—the experience of being taken apart, devoured, or torn to pieces on a global scale, allowing for a shift of awareness and transformation of collective consciousness. At its deepest level, the dismemberment experience dismantles our old identity. It is a powerful death-and-rebirth process. The experience of being stripped, layer by layer, down to bare bones forces us to examine the bare essence of what we truly are.

Anthropologist Felicitas Goodman, the modern discoverer of ritual trance and sacred postures, notes that Siberian shamans considered dismemberment to be an essential phase of initiation for healers. Goodman researched and explored ritual body postures as a means to achieve a bodily induced trance experience and discovered that this archetype appears to be universal. In her trance work with Westerners, those who experienced spontaneous dismemberment visions were invariably destined to become various kinds of healers.

Completing this restorative rite is precisely the task of the shaman. As anthropologist Joan Halifax explains in her book *Shamanic Voices*, "The shaman is a healed healer who has retrieved the broken pieces of his or her body and psyche and, through a personal rite of transformation, has integrated many planes of life experience: the body and the spirit, the ordinary and non-ordinary, the individual and the community, nature and supernature, the mythic and the historical, the past, the present and the future."[3] The cure for dismemberment is remembering who we actually are. As Halifax puts it, "To bring back to an original state that which was in primordial times whole and is now broken and dismembered is not only an act of unification, but also a divine remembrance of a time when a complete reality existed."[4]

The viewpoint emerging from the shamanic community suggests the times we live in have a theme of planetary and cosmological initiation. Shamanic initiation is most often precipitated by physical, psychological, emotional, or spiritual events that force the ego into submission. Who we believe ourselves to be is not who we truly are. No matter how many years one has been developing their consciousness, no one is exempt from this shamanic death-and-rebirth. This is a shamanic initiation on the grandest cosmological scale.

The caveat is to not swing into polar extremes of elation or trepidation. Some may view this as a golden opportunity for ultimate transformation and spiritual growth. Others may react from fear and view this as impending doom and gloom. Rather, view the melodramatic experience as a test of spiritual maturity. This provides the opportunity for letting go and surrendering our ego defensiveness.

The times we find ourselves in are like a great river in flood. We can try to hold on to the shore to save ourselves from being swept along with the current. But this is a futile effort, for nothing can resist the great tide of change that is sweeping through and forever altering life as we have known it for millennia. Instead, we are being challenged to let go and go with the flow. We are being given the opportunity to surrender to the current of change so that new dreams and visions can emerge. We can navigate these difficult times by following our deepest instincts, intuition and insights.

A Stanford University team has boldly proposed that—living as we are through the last years of one Earth epoch, and the birth of another—we belong to "Generation Anthropocene." In the Anthropocene age, we are undergoing a transition to a new realization of consciousness. The acceleration of planetary crises can either provoke a planetary awakening and a shift into a regenerative planetary culture based on shamanic wisdom and sustainable principles, or a destruction of human civilization in its current form, and perhaps extinction for our species. We are all responsible, for better or worse. We are navigators of the Anthropocene—attempting to find our way to a new home.

THE GREAT SHIFT

Chapter 2

Navigating the Great Shift

Paradise is not a place; it's a state of consciousness.
—Sri Chinmoy, Indian spiritual leader who taught meditation in the West[1]

It is not hard to see that, even though we live on a planet that surrounds us with beauty, there is a lot of darkness manifesting within humanity. We must learn to deal with this dissonant energy. We cannot make sense of it because it is entirely destructive. In these uncertain times, it is impossible to find stability in the outer world, so do not waste your time looking for it. Instead, we must hold steady within ourselves and observe the chaos from an inner place of power. When we center ourselves and calm our minds, we stop feeding the negative drama that is playing out on Earth. Our inner calm and stability helps contain the darkness so that it is unable to wreak as much havoc upon the world.

The present upheaval in our world must take place. Earth changes occur when imbalances need to be corrected. Major Earth changes are here now and you have a part to play in it. You are supposed to be on Earth at this time in history. You chose to be here because you wanted to be part of this great change. So take time each day to still your mind and go within, for the answers to all your questions lie within you. The world's great spiritual traditions teach that it is necessary to still the mind and quiet the emotions so that personal truth can emerge. Then, with truth as your guide, your actions will be in accord with the times. It can be easy to lose hope at times, yet there are many opportunities for spiritual growth and meaningful action during this time. Here are some helpful guidelines to navigate these dark and turbulent times:

Take total personal responsibility for your life

Personal responsibility is taking conscious control of how you think, act and feel in response to the events and circumstances in your life. Accept yourself and your circumstances. Accept responsibility for who you are right now. It is not other people who made you the way you are, but only your own choices, thoughts and actions. Earth has always been a free will planet. We incarnate here on Earth to experience freedom of choice. We can choose to do anything we want. There are other worlds where we learn other experiences, but the human realm is the only one in which our choices (good or bad) affect our future. We live in a reciprocally interrelated world where there are repercussions for our actions. As conscious moral agents, humans have power that the beings in other realms do not; this clearly underscores the importance of moral action and spiritual development.

See the world as it truly is

When we open our eyes, do we see the world as it really is? Do we see reality? The answer is that we do not see reality, according to new neuroscience research. In his book, *Deviate: The Science of Seeing Differently*, neuroscientist Beau Lotto tells us it is the human mind that imposes meaning on our perceptions. He thinks our perceptions terminate at the boundaries of our brain. According to Lotto, we function with versions of reality that have nothing to do with what is actually out there—what exists in the real world.

Neuroscience studies show that perception is not what our eyes and ears tell us; it is what our brain makes us see and hear. Your personal reality is not the perception of what is "out there," but an observation of what is going on inside your head. The senses are similar to the keyboard of a computer: they provide access, but the real job is done in the brain. Your brain takes in the information from your senses, but your reality is not made up of the atoms of the "real world." It is made up of the atoms of your brain. Perception is just an illusory product of our mind. The world we see around us is ultimately no more real than a hologram.

New research demonstrates that we do not see the real world; we only see what helped us to survive in the past. As Lotto puts it, "We don't see reality—we only see what was useful to see in the past."[2] Much like a road map, our perceptual brain does not offer an accurate spatial representation; rather, it helps us to navigate in a safe and efficient way. The world revealed by our senses is not the real world, but an imperfect copy of it. In our conscious mind we see the world through a distorted perception system. The world we live in does not exist in the way we perceive it. Because of this flawed information collection system we can never *see the world as it truly is*. Lotto astutely observes that, "Our species has been so successful not in spite of our inability to see reality but because of it."[3]

Perception underpins everything we think, know and believe. Yet if our perception is a manifestation of our past, how is it ever possible to step outside the past in order to live and create differently in the future? Lotto believes that deviating from the way we currently perceive will lead to future innovations in thought and behavior in all aspects of our lives. This is why the book is called *Deviate*. He argues that perception includes a lot of assumptions which contribute to preconceived ideas that keep us stuck in a narrow perspective of our personal and social reality. Lotto thinks that the next big innovation will not be a new technology but instead will be a new way of seeing.

The world that we see around us is nothing more than a very convincing illusion and can completely change in the blink of an eye. Light is the only true thing that we can see in the world. The challenge we face is that light manifests itself, as well as darkness. Consequently, there are two spiritual forces that we deal with on planet Earth everyday: light (positive) energy and dark (negative) energy. Light energy is unlimited and comes from the divine source. It is highly vibrational, expansive and full of love. Dark energy is dense, negative, and goes against the flow of the universe. It is about manipulation, oppression, conquest and fear. Darkness is part of who we are, and we all have to take responsibility for it. So no matter how hopeless the world may seem, it is only a mirage. Light is the only real thing there is. The rest is a dream.

Learn to live with your heart, not your mind

We live in a highly visual world that continually bombards us with stimulation, exposing us to a multitude of sensations that keep us in our heads. In a chaotic, rapidly changing world, it can be difficult to figure things out, so it is best to turn away from the external theatrics and move into our heart space—into the stillness at our center. It is time to shift from the intellect of the mind to the intuition of the heart and let that begin navigating our choices. Intuition reveals appropriate action in the moment for a given set of circumstances. A gut feeling is the sensation you first experience when your intuition is activated and is trying to communicate something important to you. It will often feel like a hunch or urge towards a certain action or decision. Sometimes it may even come as a whisper from your inner self.

To live fully from the heart, we must learn to still the mind so that our intuitive self can come to light. Stopping the mind's incessant chatter frees us of doubt, fear and limitation. Such inner calm and openness connects us with the guidance of our own inner knowing. Take time every day to quiet the mind, whether in meditation or prayer, and ask to be taken into your heart's sacred space. Then while you are there, practice seeing the world from that point of view. The energy that comes in from the source is directed through our hearts. When we are in sync with the heart, we are in sync with the Cosmos. As we learn to live from the heart, we are able to move with the ebb and flow of change with grace and ease. Living a heart-centered life will restore and rejuvenate you, and then you will have something to give back to the world.

Keep your heart open

One of the most important things you can do at this time is to keep your heart wide open. To keep your heart open, be willing to accept what life brings you. Regardless of the experience happening around you, how you respond, how you choose to perceive that experience is always your choice. You can use what happens to learn and grow from your experience. Resistance is futile anyway, and what you resist persists. You need a completely balanced and open heart to be able to hold steady during these dark times. Make a conscious choice not to be swept along by unfavorable circumstances or permit your steadfastness to be shaken.

You do not have total control over what happens to you—in fact, often you have no control at all. But you have considerable control over how you relate to what happens to you. You can be mindful of your feelings and hold yourself with kindness and compassion. It is important to be mindful of who you are. You are a being of light, capable of the most extraordinary things. You were put here on Earth to hold a steady place in an unsteady world. Remain calm and centered in your power. Never compromise or lose sight of your goals and principles. Such an attitude will sustain the inner light that exists within you in even the darkest of times. We each have a part to play during this dark time. We each hold a piece to the puzzle. Through honest seeking and compassionate sharing, we can weave our threads of wisdom together to create a whole tapestry.

Seek equanimity or steadiness of mind

Equanimity is the capacity to remain poised and calm even when under stress. According to Buddhist teachings, equanimity is an unshakable balance of mind. The kind of equanimity required must be rooted in the insight that we create our own reality. Nothing that happens to us comes from an external source outside ourselves; everything is the result of our own thoughts and deeds. Because this knowledge frees us from fear, it is the foundation of equanimity.

To attain equanimity as an unshakable state of mind, we must release all attachments to negative feelings and thoughts that float on the stream of mind. It requires diligence and commitment to release such attachments. The moment you feel some thought of fear, anger or doubt creeping into your mind, simply let it go. Allow it to drift off on the air of the wind, on the breath of life. Breathe deeply and gently exhale any tension you might feel. You must be gentle with yourself, in spite of your errors, and gentle with others who react from a place of fear or anger. Equanimity allows us to stand in the midst of conflict or crisis in a way where we are balanced, centered and grounded.

Stay grounded

Grounding is a technique that gets you rooted in your body and helps keep you in the present moment. It is only in the present moment that you can fully live your life. Grounding techniques are designed to redistribute the energy from your head into your body. Doing so has an almost instant calming effect. Grounding can reduce anxiety, quiet the mind and connect you to your inner voice. These simple techniques can ground you in your own truth and help you get to know your inner self. Grounding is also essential for basic health and survival. Grounding enhances your ability to function effectively on a day-to-day basis. When poorly grounded, your spatial awareness is impaired. Spatial awareness is the ability to understand and interact with the environment around you. When ungrounded, you may feel scattered, off-balance, and find yourself tripping a lot.

Grounding begins with mindful breathing. The most basic way to do mindful breathing is simply to focus on your breath as you inhale and exhale. You can do this while standing, sitting or even lying down. You can keep your eyes open, but you may find it easier to hold your focus if you close your eyes. You do not need to do anything to your breath. Just breathe naturally and focus your attention on where you feel your breath in your body. It may be in your abdomen, chest, throat or nostrils. As you do this, your mind may start to wander. This is perfectly natural. Just notice that your mind has wandered, and then gently redirect your attention back to the breathing. Stay here for five to seven minutes. It helps to set aside a designated time for mindful grounding each day.

Another fast and effective technique is simply to stand like the World Tree. Stand with your feet parallel, about six inches apart, and your toes aimed straight ahead. Your knees should be slightly bent, removing any strain on your lower back. Now stretch your arms out from your sides so that you stand as a cross-tree at the center of all things. Close your eyes and imagine that you are the World Tree standing at the very navel of the universe. Your roots tap deeply into the underworld, and your crown touches the heavens.

Get outside and enjoy nature. Try walking, gardening or just sitting under a tree. Touching a tree can help you ground and discharge negative energy from your body. Physically touching or sitting on the earth will have a calming and grounding effect. Take in the beauty of nature with all of your senses. Breathe in the colors, shapes and textures. Immerse yourself in the sights, sounds and smells. Allow the natural world to ground you in the present moment. Nature calms, helps you connect to something larger than yourself, and provides a much-needed break from your busy life. In the modern world we often get so caught up in our busy lives that we forget to honor our inherent connection with the natural world.

Cleanse yourself and your home of negative energy daily

Whether we realize it or not, we are attracting harmful energetic vibrations from our environment. Picking up negative energy that is not ours can make us less balanced and can cause blockages to the natural flow of energy in our body. We may feel tired, unbalanced, anxious, depressed or even sick. The most important thing you can do is to smudge yourself and your home each day. Smudging is a method of using smoke from burning herbs to dispel negative energy. Sage, cedar and sweetgrass are traditionally used for smudging. To smudge, light the dried herbs in a fire-resistant receptacle, and then blow out the flames. Then use a feather or your hands to fan the smoke around your body and home. I recommend cracking a window or door for ventilation and for releasing unwanted energies.

Use consecrated or holy water. The practice of charging water with intention, words, and sound is widely practiced in indigenous cultures throughout the world. In fact, people have believed in our ability to influence water since the days of antiquity. The Christian tradition is the obvious example, with the ongoing performing of rituals that turn regular water into holy water. Essentially, holy water is water with salt added during a rite of blessing. Learn how to make your own consecrated water, and use it for cleansing, protection and blessing.[4] Pour some holy water into a spray bottle. To cleanse your aura, or personal energy field, spray it toward yourself from arms length. To bless and protect your home, spray holy water around the perimeter of your dwelling and yard. Many people will dismiss the power of holy water based on its association with the church. This is not about religion; this is about a pragmatic solution to an age-old problem. The fact of the matter is that holy water is your best protection against negative and dark energies.

Practice white light cleansing. Light—imagined or real—is a powerful aura cleanser. White light can be called upon by anyone for cleansing, healing and protection from negative energies. Begin by finding somewhere that you can sit undisturbed for several minutes, and then do some mindful breathing to calm and focus your mind. Next, visualize a sphere of white light emanating from your heart. Just allow it to expand outward until it completely fills and surrounds you. Envision the white light purifying your body and displacing any negative or foreign energy. Really focus on seeing it clearly in your mind and keep building it up so it is brilliant and glowing. You can keep expanding the light, sending peace and love out into infinity.

Use protection stones. Protection stones can help dispel negative energies and shield you from psychic, emotional and physical attack. Black tourmaline repels lower, harmful frequencies and is good for general all-round protection. Black obsidian is a good grounding stone to wear in your aura each day, shielding you from negativity, sorcery and spirit attachments. Jet helps clear internalized emotional energy. Apache tears transmute negative energy. These gemstones can be obtained as small tumbled stones which can easily be carried in your pocket every day. To protect your entire home, place black obsidian in the four main corners of your house. Cleanse your stones frequently with holy water.

Establish clear personal boundaries

Establishing clear personal boundaries is the key to ensuring relationships are mutually respectful, supportive and caring. Boundaries are a measure of self-esteem. They set the limits for acceptable behavior from those around you. Weak boundaries leave you vulnerable and likely to be taken for granted or even damaged by others. Set aside some time to clearly define what your physical, emotional and spiritual boundaries are with friends, family, co-workers and strangers. Make a list of things you want people to stop doing around you, things you want people to stop doing to you, and things that people may no longer say to you.

Once you have established strong, clear boundaries, people will give you more respect. This means you can be your authentic self, asking for what you really want and need without fear of judgment. Emotional and spiritual manipulators will back off and in their place sustainable, loving relationships will thrive. Extending boundaries comes with a price, and this may be losing acquaintances along the way. Of course, those relationships that are worth having will survive and grow stronger.

As time goes on, your boundaries may require updating. It helps to identify your core values, belief system, and outlook on life so you have a clear picture of who you are and how you want to live. When linked to your core values, boundaries help you align your daily activities and behaviors with your life's purpose. The passionate expression of our soul's purpose is precisely the medicine the Earth needs at this time.

Create effective rituals and ceremonies

Ritual and ceremony are essential for a healthy and balanced personal and communal life. Many persistent personal and social problems can be linked to the lack of ritual and ceremony. Rituals and ceremonies reduce tension, anxiety and stress, produce deeper self-awareness, and connect us to our community. They connect us with our deepest core values and our highest vision of who we are and why we are here.

Ritual and ceremony are two distinct practices used to engage the powers of the unseen world. Ceremony is a formal act or set of acts designed to celebrate, honor or acknowledge what is. Ceremony is used to strengthen or restore the status quo, grounding people in the natural order of things and/or deepening communal relationships. In essence, though the actions and performance of a ceremony may recognize and/or acknowledge an effect, it does not produce an effect on its own. The purpose of ceremony is to bring people together on a specific occasion.

Ritual is a formal act or set of acts designed to cause a change in what is—to change or transform the status quo. Where a ceremony simply bids a blessing or presence from a higher power, a ritual more often asks for favor or intercession of some form. The purpose of ritual is to engage the spirit world to effect specific changes in the physical world.

Ritual and ceremony are a universal way to address the spirit world and provide some kind of fundamental change in an individual's consciousness or in the ambience of a gathering. They may involve prayers, chanting, drumming, dancing, anointing, as well as rites of passage. Both are designed to engage the spirit world in helping us to do what we are unable to do for ourselves. Without the connection to the powers of the spirit world, neither is an effective tool for restoring or changing the status quo. By creating effective ritual and ceremony, we can skillfully engage spirit in the processes we are involved in like healing, therapy or actualizing our goals. Potent rituals and ceremonies have similar foundational elements. Key elements of this foundation include:

1. Intention is the first element of effective ritual and ceremony. You should have a clear idea of what you want to accomplish. Without a clear intention or desired outcome, the energy created in the ritual or ceremony is poorly structured with little or no direction. Articulating your desired outcome is how you channel the energy of the performance toward the intended objective. One good way to think about it is by asking yourself what you want to happen as a result of the ritual or ceremony. What effect do you want it to have on individuals, community and the world?

2. The creation of sacred space. Sacred space is that territory that we enter for spiritual and inner work. Regardless of your spiritual beliefs, having a special place in your home reserved for quiet introspection, reflection and spiritual connection can nourish your soul. A sacred space can be any location in your home where you can be by yourself and be fully self-expressed. Be creative with this, but find a special place for you to go at least once a day.

Consider setting up an altar that is appropriate for the purpose of your ritual or ceremony. Although an altar is not essential, it provides us with a focus to pray, meditate and listen. An altar is any structure upon which we place offerings and sacred objects that have spiritual or cosmological significance. It represents the center and axis of your sacred space. A simple altar can be created with a cloth, a candle and other symbols that mean something to you.

It is important to cleanse your sacred space before starting any spiritual work. Cleanse the space by smudging and/or spraying holy water around the perimeter. Preparing a purified sacred space shifts our awareness from ordinary waking consciousness to a more centered, meditative state. Ritual preparation awakens our connection to the web of life and structures a boundary that separates the sacred from the ordinary and profane.

3. The opening of sacred space. After preparing a purified sacred space, you may wish to ritually open the space. The opening of sacred space is essentially an invocation; calling in the spiritual energies of the seven directions: East, South, West, North, Up, Down and Within. Calling in the directions not only aligns you with their power, but is a spiritual activity in and of itself. The orientation embeds you in the living web of life, yielding greater awareness and perspective. It imparts a comprehensive recollection of the basic experience of being fully human. The ritual grounds you completely in the present moment to begin your day or to begin a specific spiritual practice.

Though there are no rules or restrictions, on most occasions a sacred circle is cast in a sun-wise direction. I would suggest you start in the East where the sun rises. If you have a rattle, shake it four times to open a portal in the East to the spirit world. Rattles are used to invoke the assistance of benevolent helping spirits. The rattle draws the spirit world and its inhabitants into the material world. Using words, chanting or song, invite the benevolent spirit powers associated with that direction to participate and assist in the ritual or ceremony. Welcome the spirits with an open heart and mind. Some people will whistle or make animal sounds to call in spirit helpers. Trust your instincts and intuition in this process.

Pause after calling the spirit helpers of the East and listen for any guidance or wisdom that direction has to share. The spirits will always respond when you call them. Sound does not just travel out into oblivion. There is a call and then a response. Pay attention to any guidance that comes to you. Communication may enter your awareness as a flash of color in your mind's eye, a visual symbol, a tingling of the spine or an inaudible sound heard deep within your soul. It may be visual, auditory, intuitive or some combination of these. Sometimes it is just a knowing that your helping spirits and guides are now around you. You may feel energy flowing into your hands, feet or arms, or showering down through your crown. When I channel spirit energy, I often feel chills and goose-bumps.

Next, pivot around clockwise and repeat the same procedure to invoke the spirits of the South, the West and the North. After that, invoke Father Sky above and Mother Earth below. When invoking Father Sky, reach to the heavens; when invoking Mother Earth, reach down and touch the ground where you stand.

Finally, face the center of the circle and bring your hands to your heart to invite the spirit of Within. Call upon the spirit of divine unity that flows from within the center of your being where the six directions meet. Welcome the gifts of balance, oneness and connection with all things, for all things are one and all things are related. At this point, the process becomes either a ritual or ceremony depending on the intention.

4. The induction of altered states. Altered states of consciousness are induced through intense rhythmic stimulation such as drumming, chanting and dancing. An altered state of consciousness is any state of mind that is significantly different from normal waking consciousness. Altered states produce deeper self-awareness; allow us to connect with the power of the universe, to externalize our own knowledge and to internalize our answers.

5. The closure of sacred space. When you have finished your ritual or ceremony, sacred space should be closed. Follow the same procedure as for the opening, but in reverse order. Begin by thanking the spiritual energies of Within, Mother Earth and Father Sky, and then the North, West, South and East in a counterclockwise movement. Shake your rattle to say farewell to the spirits. As you rattle, give thanks to all your relations for the needs met. The phrase "all my relations" is used at the end of a prayer in many shamanic traditions, for all living things share in the relationships of life on Earth. Express your gratitude to the helping spirits for assisting you and send them off, releasing their energies to the seven directions.

Pray without ceasing

The word prayer is derived from the two Sanskrit words *pra* and *artha* meaning pleading fervently. In other words, it is asking God (or whatever term you would like to use for a higher power) for something with intense yearning. To pray without ceasing means to be continually in a reverent attitude of prayer. Regular prayer is a cornerstone of spiritual practice.

Over time, frequent prayers help to dissolve our mind and through them we gain access to divine consciousness. Praying brings us divine help, reduces our ego, grants us forgiveness of mistakes, and more. Prayer does not have to be complex or eloquent; just simple and sincere from the heart.

The power of prayer should never be underestimated. Words have great power. In the shamanic world, words transform substance. I am now going to tell you about one of the most powerful phrases in the human language. Simply begin your prayer with the words, "In the name of Jesus, I pray." This prayer is so simple, yet so powerful. Praying in the name of Jesus invokes his power and protects us from darkness. It is his job to take evil away. If you put Jesus between you and anything dark, that dark cannot touch you. Again, this is not about religion; this is about a pragmatic approach that works. It is about speaking words that liberate us from the power of darkness. The reason this prayer is so powerful is that the name of Jesus is not just a passive word. It is a creative word of power that makes possible the things that it commands.

Learn how to make prayer ties

The sacrament tobacco is used cross-culturally as a unifying thread of communication between humans and the spiritual powers. Offering tobacco smoke or a pinch of dry tobacco carries our prayers to the "Loom of Creation," thereby reweaving the pattern of existence in accordance with those prayers. Prayer ties are spiritual offerings created by wrapping tobacco into a cloth while praying and focusing on an intention—what you desire or expect to accomplish. They should be thought of as a physical manifestation of your prayer.

A prayer tie is made with a small (about 2 inches) square of 100% cotton cloth and it is usually tied with 100% cotton string. The cotton cloth is usually red, but can be of any color, depending on the circumstances, which tradition you are following, or what your intuition tells you. To make a prayer tie, begin by smudging yourself and your materials. After smudging, take a pinch of tobacco and focus on your intention while holding it. Next, place the pinch of tobacco at the center of the cloth. Gather the four corners of the fabric together and pinch at the top, forming a small pouch. Loop the string around the pouch and tie it up tight. If you are making more than one prayer tie, space them evenly on the string. I usually make a tobacco tie for each of the seven directions: East, South, West, North, Up, Down and Within.

Creating a small sacred bundle to hold the tobacco makes it easier to carry on your person, to make an offering to another person, and to hold on to for longer periods of time. As with any sacred object, treat your prayer ties with the honor and respect they deserve. Upon completion, prayer tie offerings might be left hanging in a tree, buried in the ground, left on a mountain top, added to your sacred space, or offered to grandfather fire. When prayer ties are ritually burned, they open a path of communication between the human world and the spirit world.

There are many good reasons for making prayer ties. Everyone should make personal prayer ties, and then carry them at all times for protection from negativity. To protect your home from negative or unwanted energies, you should hang a string of prayer ties over each entry door to your dwelling. Prayer ties can be placed on altars or attached to sacred objects like drums. The making of prayer ties is a wonderful way to prepare for ceremonies such as sweat lodge, vision quest, or whenever there is a sacred fire. Creating prayer ties is a good way to pray for the safe passage of newly deceased souls. Giving a tobacco tie to someone who has helped you is a good way to show your appreciation for what they have done for you and how much you value their friendship.

Experience the power of chanting

Chanting is prayer. In ancient times, chant was the closest thing to dialogue with the spirit. There are chants to honor the dead, to pay homage to deities, or to invoke qualities such as wisdom, compassion and empathy. Given our contemporary hectic lifestyles, chanting is the most conducive path of spiritual practice for the times we live in. Chanting has no limitations of time and space and can be done anytime or anywhere. Chanting as a spiritual practice helps to foster maximum spiritual growth and overall well-being. It is a simple and effortless way to still the mind and bring deep relaxation to the body. It is an effective way to open the heart and connect with a higher power.

Many chants are mantras—single words or phrases repeated over and over. Mantras are indestructible positive energies, meaning they remain in the universe indefinitely for the greater good of all. One of the most simple and powerful mantras we can chant is the sound of OM, the primal sound from which the universe constantly emanates. Chanting the mantra OM attunes us to the eternal oneness of all that is, unifying body, mind and spirit. When pronouncing OM, it should sound like "home" without the "h" sound. When chanting OM, equal measure should be given to both the "O" and the "M" sounds (i.e., oooommmm). Take in a deep breath and voice the sound as you exhale through the mouth. When chanted with love, devotion and sincerity, the positive effects are greatly accentuated.

Give thanks

Giving thanks and being in a state of gratitude opens our heart, allowing our indwelling presence of being, our spirit, to rise forth unimpeded. Gratitude, like any other spiritual practice, is something we do, not just something we feel. And it is something we need to practice. Try to cultivate a spirit of gratitude in all things. Even in situations that seem difficult to give thanks for, just remember that you are on the Earth to experience, learn and grow. An "attitude of gratitude" in all things helps connect us to our core values and purpose for being here.

Foster a reciprocal relationship of meaning to the Earth. Take time to honor and respect the reciprocal cycle of give and take, for Mother Earth provides everything we need to live and flourish. Express your gratitude through prayer and offerings. Give thanks also for the things you are praying for. Giving thanks before needs are met is a way of making space to receive them. Reciprocity is the guiding principle of the indigenous shamanic path. We can restore balance to the planet. We humans have all the necessary talents to be reciprocal caretakers of Mother Earth.

Develop a spiritual practice

The most important thing you can do at this time is to develop a spiritual practice. A spiritual practice is the regular performance of actions and activities undertaken for the purpose of inducing spiritual experiences and cultivating spiritual development. A spiritual practice is something you do every single day that facilitates deeper self-awareness, empathy and connectedness with others. Regular spiritual practice fosters inner peace, insight, compassion, non-attachment, integration and a sense of unity. Consistent spiritual practice helps to build spiritual strength and this in turn becomes our protective armor. We must not fall into hopelessness, but instead must strengthen our personal practice and act as a light in dark times for those around us that are lost.

Ultimately, spiritual practice leads to self-realization or enlightenment. It is important to remember that each person is different, so what works for one person may not work for another. The key is to choose an activity that makes you feel calm, centered and relaxed. A spiritual activity might be dancing, drumming, chanting, meditating, praying, doing yoga or tai chi. Any behavior that is kind, gentle, generous, virtuous, sincere, respectful and reverent brings us closer to the next stage in the cycle, a Golden Age of primeval peace, harmony and prosperity.

10 good reasons to develop a spiritual practice

1. To improve health and quality of life: Contemplative practice can promote calm and clarity as well as improve cognitive functions. Brain research shows that meditation rebuilds the brain's gray matter, which can improve learning and memory, enhance immune system function, help regulate emotions and relieve stress. Studies show that chanting reduces heart rate and blood pressure while boosting immunity, memory and focus. Prayer induces relaxation, along with feelings of hope, gratitude, empathy and compassion—all of which increase overall well-being. Ritual and ceremony reduce stress, increase self-awareness, and connect us to our community. An exhaustive review that compared spirituality to other health interventions found that people with a strong spiritual life had an 18% reduction in mortality.
2. To connect with the intuitive self: It is necessary to still the mind and quiet the emotions so that insight and intuition can emerge into our consciousness. Buddhism teaches that we have to achieve a state of "no-thought;" and Taoism teaches that we have to achieve a state of "non-doing." Inner stillness quells the ego and connects us to the guidance of our own intuitive knowing. Right action appears within consciousness as the most natural thing to do. One can readily perceive what aims are in accord with the Cosmos and not waste energy on discordant pursuits. By allowing the intuition to lead the body, one attains clarity in movement. So long as we follow our intuitive sense, our actions will be in sync with the true self and ultimately the Cosmos.
3. To explore and develop the inner life: Spiritual practice makes us more fluent in the language of the inner life, which is where meaningful

healing, transformation and insight arise. Being mindfully present with our thoughts, feelings and sensations is a journey into deeper self-awareness. Regardless of what you call it—personal growth, personal development, self-actualization, or finding yourself—this journey is you exploring and developing who you truly are.

4. To broaden our perspective: Spiritual practice affords a holistic view of life on a macrocosmic level. Spiritual practice is a valuable tool for stepping back and getting a balanced perspective on the broader picture. When we become fixated on the chaos, violence and cruelties taking place in the world, we lose perspective. We must take the long view if we are going to truly see. Any time we set out to change our lives or the world, we have to take the long view. Through regular, consistent spiritual practice, we gain the perspective needed to move with the ebb and flow of change with grace and ease.

5. To achieve joy and bliss: A daily spiritual practice is the surest path to bliss and joy. Joy is our song which we share with the universe. Every living thing has a unique song, a pulsing rhythm that belongs only to it. Within the heart of each of us, there exists a silent pulse of perfect rhythm that connects us to the totality of a dynamic, interrelated universe. This silent pulse is ever-present within each of us, but our awareness is rarely in sync with it. Awareness of perfect rhythm is not possible until we relinquish the desires and manipulations of the ego.

6. In order to focus our attention: Spiritual practice cultivates the attention required to complete our tasks and improve the quality of our experience. As Mihaly Csikszentmihalyi, a positive psychologist best known for his theory of flow, points out in his book, *Flow: The Psychology of Optimal Experience*, "The shape and content of life depend on how attention has been used…attention is our most important tool in the task of improving the quality of experience…attention shapes the self, and is in turn shaped by it."[5] So how do we get to this optimal state of consciousness called flow? We get there by focusing intently on an activity. Csikszentmihalyi defines flow as "the state in which people are so involved in an activity that nothing else seems to matter; the experience itself is so enjoyable that people will do it even at great cost, for the sheer sake of doing it."[6]

7. To raise your vibration: Cruelty, violence and instability are on the rise. To raise the heavy vibration of fear that is enveloping the world, lift your own vibration. Do this with drumming, chanting and prayer.

Repetitive drumming, chanting and prayer cleanse the aura, boost the immune system and produce feelings of well-being, a release of emotional trauma, and reintegration of self.

8. To develop divine qualities: We are all sparks of the same one divine source. Over time, spiritual practice helps to dissolve our mind and through it we gain access to divine consciousness. This closeness to divinity allows us to assimilate divine attributes and evolve spiritually. Through our efforts to develop divine qualities in ourselves, such as love, kindness, forgiveness, gratitude, acceptance, compassion and empathy, we become a beacon of light for others.

9. To achieve clarity of mind: Buddhism teaches that the purpose of contemplative practice is to increase clarity and awareness by clearing the mind of illusions and obstructions. By increasing our clarity and awareness, right practice makes it so our view becomes more right. As our view becomes more right, our thought becomes more right. As our thought becomes more right, our actions become more right, creating a feedback loop of continuous improvement.

10. To ground ourselves fully in the present moment: The present moment is all you ever have. When you are not present in the moment, you become a victim of time. Your mind is pulled into the past or the future, or both. Make now the primary focus of your life. The present moment is the fundamental ceremony of life. When we bring ourselves fully into the present moment, our life becomes the spiritual practice.

THE GREAT SHIFT

Chapter 3

Harnessing the Power of Drumming

Yes; there is a Spirit in the body of the drum carved out of the trunk of a tree; there is a Spirit in the skin of the drum itself. All this, plus the Spirit of the person playing the drum, becomes an irresistible force against any immovable object.
—Babatunde Olatunji, Nigerian drummer, activist and recording artist[1]

Drumming is a spiritual practice that can help us heal and restore ourselves and our communities. It is one of the quickest and most powerful ways I know to open the heart and connect with a power greater than ourselves. The drum is a time-tested vehicle for healing and self-expression. It can be used to address any number of health issues including trauma, addiction, depression and chronic pain. Recent research reviews indicate that drumming accelerates physical healing, boosts the immune system and produces feelings of well-being, a release of emotional trauma and reintegration of self.

Other studies have demonstrated the calming, focusing and healing effects of drumming on Alzheimer's patients, autistic children, combat veterans, emotionally disturbed teens, recovering addicts, trauma patients, and prison and homeless populations. Study results demonstrate that drumming is a valuable treatment for stress, fatigue, anxiety, addiction, hypertension, asthma, chronic pain, arthritis, heart disease, mental illness, cancer, multiple sclerosis, Parkinson's disease, stroke, emotional disorders and a wide range of physical disabilities.

Additionally, shamanic techniques such as journeying, shapeshifting and divination can all be performed with the drum. According to Mariko Namba Walter and Eva Jane Neumann Fridman, authors of *Shamanism: An Encyclopedia of World Beliefs, Practices, and Culture*, "The drum is used in a variety of ways in shamanist rituals; it may serve as (1) a rhythm instrument, (2) a divination table, (3) a 'speaker' for communicating with the spirits, (4) a spirit-catcher, (5) a spirit boat, (6) a purifying device, (7) the shaman's mount."[2]

Drumming for mindfulness and healing

Drumming is perhaps the oldest form of meditation known to humanity. It is a simple and effortless way to still the mind, thereby inducing altered states of consciousness. A significant number of research studies have documented both drumming and mindfulness meditation as effective therapy for everything from stress to depression to supportive cancer treatment. This is not new science. Since the time of Buddha (about 2,600 years ago), we have known about the stress-reducing benefits of both drumming and mindfulness meditation, which focuses on nonjudgmental awareness of sensations, feelings and state of mind.

Combining these two ancient practices—drumming and mindfulness—can be life-altering. Mindful drumming could not be simpler: take a good seat, focus on the beat, and when your attention wanders, return. Even one session of mindful drumming demonstrates how powerful this meditation method can be in our stressful modern lives. The powerful and compelling rhythm of the drum can still and focus the mind—the fast path to mindfulness and well-being.

The neuroscience of drumming

According to new neuroscience research, rhythm is rooted in innate functions of the brain, mind and consciousness. As human beings, we are innately rhythmic. Our relationship with rhythm begins in the womb. At twenty-two days, a single (human embryo) cell jolts to life. This first beat awakens nearby cells and incredibly they all begin to beat in perfect unison. These beating cells divide and become our heart. This desire to beat in unison seemingly fuels our entire lives. Studies show that, regardless of musical training, we are innately able to perceive and recall elements of beat and rhythm.

It makes sense, then, that beat and rhythm are an important aspect in music therapy. Our brains are hard-wired to be able to entrain to a beat. Entrainment occurs when two or more rhythms come into sync and begin to beat as one. If you are walking down a street and you hear a song, you instinctively begin to step in sync to the beat of the song. This is actually an important area of current music therapy research. Our brain enables our motor system to naturally entrain to a rhythmic beat, allowing music therapists to target rehabilitating movements. Rhythm is a powerful gateway to well-being.

Neurologic drum therapy

Neuroscience research has demonstrated the therapeutic effects of rhythmic drumming. The reason rhythm is such a powerful tool is that it permeates the entire brain. Vision, for example, is in one part of the brain, speech another, but drumming accesses the whole brain. The sound of drumming generates dynamic neuronal connections in all parts of the brain even where there is significant damage or impairment, such as in Attention Deficit Disorder. According to Michael Thaut, director of Colorado State University's Center for Biomedical Research in Music, "Rhythmic cues can help retrain the brain after a stroke or other neurological impairment, as with Parkinson's patients ...."[3] The more connections that can be made within the brain, the more integrated our experiences become.

Studies indicate that drumming produces deeper self-awareness by inducing synchronous brain activity. The physical transmission of rhythmic energy to the brain synchronizes the two cerebral hemispheres, integrating conscious and unconscious awareness. When the logical left hemisphere comes into sync with the intuitive right hemisphere, intuitive knowing can flow unimpeded into our conscious awareness. The ability to access unconscious information through symbols and imagery facilitates psychological integration and a reintegration of self.

In his scholarly book, *Shamanism: The Neural Ecology of Consciousness and Healing*, Dr. Michael Winkelman reports that drumming also synchronizes the frontal and lower areas of the brain, integrating nonverbal information from lower brain structures into the frontal cortex, producing "feelings of insight, understanding, integration, certainty, conviction, and truth, which surpass ordinary understandings and tend to persist long after the experience, often providing foundational insights for religious and cultural traditions."[4]

It requires abstract thinking and the interconnection between symbols, concepts and emotions to process unconscious information. The human adaptation to translate an inner experience into meaningful narrative is uniquely exploited by drumming. Rhythmic drumming targets memory, perception and the complex emotions associated with symbols and concepts: the principal functions humans rely on to formulate belief.

Because of this exploit, the result of the synchronous brain activity in humans is the spontaneous generation of meaningful information which is imprinted into memory. Drumming is an effective method for integrating subjective experience into one's sense of self, which encourages positive attitudes and behaviors that are linked to health and well-being.

Shamanic drumming

Shamanic drumming is drumming for the purpose of inducing a range of ecstatic trance states in order to connect with the spiritual dimension of reality. Practiced in diverse cultures around the planet, this drum method is strikingly similar the world over. Shamanic drumming uses a repetitive rhythm that begins slowly and then gradually builds in intensity to a tempo of three to seven beats per second. The ascending tempo will induce light to deep trance states and facilitate the shamanic techniques of journeying, shapeshifting and divination. Practitioners use intention and discipline to control the nature, depth, and qualities of their trance experience. They may progress through a series of trance states until they reach the level that is necessary for healing to occur. When ready to exit the trance state, the practitioner simply slows the tempo of drumming, drawing consciousness back to normal. Shamanic drumming continues to offer today what it has offered for thousands of years: namely, a simple and effective technique of ecstasy.

An active meditation

The first thing you might ask is how does a drum induced trance differ from a traditional meditation, such as those practiced by Buddhists? The two forms differ absolutely in their approach, because Buddhist-type sitting meditation is generally about emptying oneself of thought, while shamanic drumming is very active and filled with content. Just like a yogi or a monk, who exists in a spiritual state most of the time because of constant devotional practices, we can readily induce profound states of deep meditation and heightened awareness by using a drum as an aid to meditation. This ease of meditation with a drum contrasts significantly with the often long periods of isolation and practice required by many other meditative disciplines before significant effects are experienced.

A bridge to the spirit world

In oral/aural cultures, sound is regarded as one of the most effective ways of establishing connections with the spirit realm since it travels through space, permeates visual and physical barriers, and conveys information from the unseen world that underlies our physical reality. Tuvan shamans of Siberia believe that the spirits of nature create their own sound world, and it is possible for humans to communicate with them through the sound of the drum. A ritual performance often begins with heating the drumhead over a fire to bring it up to the desired pitch. Shamans may strike certain parts of the drum to summon particular benevolent helping spirits who give them knowledge and assistance. It is the subtle variations in timbre and ever-changing overtones of the drum that allow the shaman to communicate with the spiritual realm. The shaman uses the drum to create a bridge to the spirit world while simultaneously opening the awareness of all the participants to that bridge.

Acoustic communication

Ritual music is a universal way to address the spirit world and provide some kind of fundamental change in an individual's consciousness or in the ambience of a gathering. All elements of drum music such as timbre, rhythm, volume and tempo play an important role in a shamanic ritual performance. By using different parts of the drumstick to play on different parts of the drum, different timbres can be produced for transmitting different meanings. Different rhythms transmit different meanings and enable the shaman to contact different beings in different realms of the Cosmos. Volume and tempo arouse feelings in the listener and communicate symbolic meanings directly as aural sense experience.

Rhythm healing

The key to understanding the shaman's world is to realize that the universe is made of vibrational energy. According to quantum physics, everything in the universe, from the smallest subatomic particle to the largest star, has an inherent vibrational pattern. The entire universe is created through vibration and can be influenced through the vibrations of shamanic drumming. The shamanic drum is a tool for altering the vibrational state of the shaman and/or the healee or a particular situation in the community. To put it simply, shamanic drumming is an ancient form of rhythm healing.

Rhythm healing is an approach that uses therapeutic rhythm techniques to promote health and well-being. Rhythm healing employs specialized rhythmic drumming patterns designed to influence the internal rhythmic patterns of the individual and harmonize those which are thought to be causing the illness or imbalance. When administered correctly, specific rhythms may be used to accelerate physical healing, stimulate the release of emotional trauma and produce deeper self-awareness. This technique has been used for thousands of years by indigenous cultures around the planet to treat a variety of conditions.

Rhythm healing relies on the natural laws of resonance and entrainment to restore the vibrational integrity of body, mind and spirit. In resonance, the sound waves produced by the drum impart their energy to the resonating systems of the body, mind and spirit, making them vibrate in sympathy. When we drum, our living flesh, brainwaves and auric energy field entrain to the sound waves and rhythms. This sympathetic resonance forms new harmonic alignments, opens the body's energy meridians, releases blocked emotional patterns, promotes healing, and helps connect us to our core, enhancing our sense of empowerment and stimulating our creative expression. A single-headed frame or hoop drum works best for rhythm healing—the larger the drum, the greater the resonance.

Finding the right rhythm

A rhythm healer may have a repertory of established rhythms or improvise a new rhythm, uniquely indicated for the situation. Determining the right rhythm in each case is a highly individual matter. No predetermined formulas are given. The rhythmist needs to create a dialogue between the sounds he/she produces and the responses of the person being treated. The drumming is not restricted to a regular tempo, but may pause, speed up or slow down with irregular accents. The practitioner may stop playing altogether, or suddenly hoist the drum skyward and bang it violently, throwing the disease into the heavens, returning it to the spirit world.

Tuvan shamans, for example, often improvise sounds, rhythms and chants in order to converse with both the spirit world and the healee. The sounds produced by the shaman and the drum go out and certain frequencies and overtones are then reflected back. Information is generally received as subtle vibrations, which the shaman then interprets as sounds, images or as rhythms.

To find the right rhythm, invoke the spirit of your drum, and ask it to come to you and become your ally. State your intention—what you desire or expect to accomplish—in a clear and concise manner, and then sit and meditate with your drum for a few minutes. By stilling the mind, you will be able to connect with the spirit of the drum. When you feel ready, pick up your drumstick and begin to play whatever feels appropriate. When you focus on the spiritual intention or the energy of what is being played, it allows the music to become very loose, spontaneous and innovative.

I learned that when I trust my intuition to play the appropriate rhythm, which I do not know in advance, I cannot go wrong. I know that when I open up and play what I feel, the drumming is fresh, different and spontaneous each time. Rhythmic improvisation is a musical expression of the soul. It is a way to let spirit work through you for the purpose of healing and helping others.

Rhythm healing is about finding the right rhythm. Rhythm and resonance order the natural world. Dissonance and disharmony arise only when we limit our capacity to resonate completely with the rhythms of life. The origin of the word rhythm is Greek meaning "to flow." We can learn to flow with the rhythms of life by simply learning to feel the beat or pulse while drumming. It is a way of bringing the essential self into accord with the flow of a boundless, interrelated universe, helping us feel connected rather than isolated and estranged.

The soul of rhythm

Every rhythm has its own quality and touches you in a unique way. These qualities, in fact, exist within each of us, longing to be activated. It is this process of internalization that allows us to access the inaudible yet perceptible soul, so to speak, of a rhythm. One of the paradoxes of rhythm is that the audible pattern is the inverse of the "inaudible matrix." Every rhythm has both an inaudible and audible aspect—silence and sound.

Silence and sound are the two fundamental aspects of our vibrational world. Silence is the unmanifest essence of the unseen world. Audible sound is the manifest form. It is the inaudible intervals between audible beats that allow us to hear the grouping of beats in a coherent cycle or pattern. We sense the interval as the offbeat, or light element, and the audible beat as the heavy element. The drummer establishes the audible beat, whereas the silent pulse quality unfolds by itself in any rhythmic pattern.

Experiencing rhythms in the body

At this time, it would be beneficial for the reader to experience how the body responds to different rhythms. Whether you drum or merely tap your fingers, learn to feel the beat by allowing it to sink into your body and consciousness. Notice how your body responds to each pattern. Keep in mind that the manner in which you play or shape a rhythm will affect your response.

Begin by playing a steady, metronome-like rhythm with uniform time intervals. A clockwork drum beat generates yang energy, which is electric, expansive and dynamic in nature. Yang energy is an ascending force conducive to initiating movement and change. At a rapid tempo of three to four beats per second, a steady, rhythmic pattern, or "eagle-beat," will arouse and vitalize you. It creates the sensation of inner movement which, if you allow it, will carry you along. As you continue to drum, you will become more ecstatic. You and your drum will seem to merge. You may speed up or slow down. That is perfectly normal. Shamanic trance is characterized by its range and flexibility, so do not be concerned with trying to maintain a certain speed. It can be distracting and your hands may get tired. Follow your inner sense of timing as to both tempo and duration.

After drumming the eagle-beat, simply relax and bathe in the sonic afterglow of physical and spiritual well-being. When the final drumbeat fades into silence, an inaudible, yet perceptible pulsation persists for a brief period. This silent pulse is ever-present within each of us, yet our awareness is rarely in sync with it. Sense this silent pulse resonating within your body. You may experience the sensation of every particle in your body pulsing in sync with the rhythm you just played. This inner pulse entrains to the rhythmic pattern as soon as you begin to drum.

Next, try playing the steady pulse of a heartbeat rhythm. A two-beat rhythm produces a different sonic experience. The familiar lub-dub, lub-dub of a heartbeat rhythm has an integrative, calming and centering effect. It reconnects us to the warmth and safety of the first sound we ever heard—the steady, nurturing pulse of our mother's heartbeat. According to Ted Andrews, author of *Animal Speak*, "a rhythm of two is a rhythm that helps connect you to the feminine energies of creative imagination, birth, and intuition."[5] The heartbeat rhythm stimulates a downward flow of energy within the body. It generates yin energy, which is magnetic, receptive and passive in nature. Yin energy is a descending force conducive to great healing and regenerative powers.

These two simple drum patterns are the healing rhythms I use most often in my shamanic work. Moreover, they are rhythm archetypes representing yin, the receptive, feminine form-giving principle of energy; and yang, the creative, masculine principle of life and consciousness immanent in all phenomena. Yin and yang are the binary elements that generate between them the totality of existence. A binary progression underlies the structure of reality. At a fundamental level, the laws of the universe are written in a binary code. The binary mathematical system forms the basis of computer languages and applies to nearly everything from crystalline structures to the genetic code. The binary basis of the genetic code is formed by the plus and minus strands of DNA (deoxyribonucleic acid).

The human experience is a microcosm and reflection of binary progression. The archetypes of rhythm are the fundamental patterns that underlie our resonant field of reality. By entraining to these archetypal rhythms, we experience them directly and discover our rhythmic interconnections. Each pattern pulsates specific qualities of energy that give inherent structure and meaning to the possibilities of being. They exist in every human being from the moment of conception to the final breath. Each human being is an integral composite of the archetypes of rhythm. Each of us is a series of rhythmic patterns summed up as a single inner pulse, the essential aspect of our being.

Selecting a drum

One of the most useful drums for shamanic work is the hand or frame drum. The frame drum originated in Siberia, together with shamanism itself thousands of years ago. It has been associated worldwide with the practice of shamanism. The frame drum's resonance and versatility make it my drum of preference. Such drums are portable, affordable and easy to play. They can easily be held in one hand, leaving the other hand free to stroke the drum. They are made by lacing wet rawhide over a wooden hoop, then allowing it to dry slowly. The hoop or frame is typically three inches or less in width and may vary from eight to twenty-four inches in diameter. They may be single-headed or double-headed. Like all rawhide drums, they do not have a fixed pitch. Heating and cooling the drumhead raises and lowers the tone.

Though I highly recommend frame drums, any type of drum may be used in shamanic drumming. There is a myriad of styles and drum types to choose from. Congas, doumbeks, djembes, ashikos, tablas and timbales are but a few of the drum types readily available in music stores. In selecting a suitable drum, play several and listen for the drum that calls to you. You will know it by its voice. It will strike a deep chord within you.

Making a drum

Another possibility is to make your own drum. To guide you in drum making, I highly recommend the book, *How to Make Drums, Tomtoms, and Rattles* by Bernard S. Mason.[6] Crafting and playing a drum that you have made yourself is eminently more satisfying than playing any other. A drum of your own creation will be imbued with your own unique essence. It will become a powerful extension of your essential self. Moreover, the spirit of a drum will pass through your hands into the drum as you make it. As master drum maker Judith Thompson put it, "Making a drum is like pulling your heart together and giving birth to a new part of yourself."[7]

Keep in mind that your drumstick or beater has a spirit and sound of its own. The best beaters for frame drums are made of strong hardwood with a padded, leather covered head. You can decorate your beater with fur, feathers, beadwork, or engrave sacred symbols into it. Different beaters work better with different drums to bring out the tone qualities. There are hard beaters, semi-hard beaters, soft beaters and rattle beaters, which are simply beaters with a rawhide or gourd rattle attached to the base of the handle opposite the head. The sound of the rattle beater draws the attention of the spirits.

Playing your drum

From a shamanic perspective, drums are living beings, helping spirits and allies. Before shamanizing with a drum, sit and meditate with the instrument for a few minutes. By quieting and centering the mind, you will be able to connect with the spirit of the drum. When you feel ready, pick up your drumstick and grip it with the thumb at the side and the fingers curled underneath. Hold the stick with a firm, relaxed grip and start playing at the rhythm the spirits direct you to use. Remember to "stroke" the drum, rather than "beat" it. Never vent your frustrations by pounding on a drum. It is better to "drum the beat" than to "beat the drum."

Always begin a drumming session by softly stroking the drum, and then gradually increase the intensity of your playing. To bring out a drum's unique voice and resonance, it is best to stroke the drum firmly, producing ringing tones and overtones. Use short strokes with a minimal amount of motion to pull the sound out of the drum. Keep your arms and shoulders relaxed, breathing slowly and deeply as you play. By playing the drum in this manner, you will have greater precision and endurance.

When a stick hits a drumhead, it rebounds in the opposite direction. The drummer who plays with too much tension, or hammers the stick into the drum, will find that the direction of the stick continues to move downward contrary to the upward push of the rebound. Rather than bouncing off the head, the stick is forced into the head by a hand still pushing down on the stick after it should have changed direction. The result is a loss of speed, control and clean, distinct strokes.

The less tension there is in the muscles of the arms and hands, the easier it is to respond to the bounce off the head. Moreover, by incorporating the energy coming off the drumhead into the upstroke, the drummer's playing will become quicker, more fluid and relaxed. That way the energy circulates, comes back and you can use it again. The key is to focus your energy to that point on the drumhead's surface that you are striking, not beyond it. Transfer your energy and intention into the drum, using a smooth, relaxed stroke. With practice, you learn just how much energy to send out to achieve a desired result and how much to retain so that you do not tire.

Move the drumstick around the head of the drum as you play, allowing the various tones and overtones to resonate through you. You will find the higher tones around the outer edges of the drumhead and the deeper sounds toward the center of the drum. If you can, find the sweet spot—that place where the drum begins to hum and sing. The drum needs to sing in order to reach its full potential for healing and empowerment.

When playing a drum, life force energy flows between the drumhead and the drumstick. With practice, you should be able to feel this subtle force pushing and pulling on the stick. Allow this force to guide your drumming in order to draw out what is already within the drum. Shamanic drumming is about transposing already existing harmonics into sound by stroking them from the drum.

Harnessing the power of the drum circle

Indigenous cultures have been practicing community percussion for thousands of years. Although most of us did not grow up in an indigenous rhythmic musical tradition, we can still tap into the healing power of the drum circle. The shamanic drum circle is the most powerful way I know to connect with the spirit and oneness of everything. Drum circles provide the opportunity for people of like mind to unite for the attainment of a shared objective. There is power in drumming alone, but that power recombines and multiplies on many simultaneous levels in a group of drummers. The drums draw individual energies together, unifying them into a consolidated force that can be channeled toward the circle's intended objective.

Drum circle participants should play in unison so that the drumming creates a mesmerizing effect to induce trance. Avoid free form drumming, which produces a cacophony of competing beats. The goal is to produce a sound that is unifying and consciousness-shifting, so individuals should alternate the responsibility of setting the tempo and leading the drum circle. Like the indigenous shaman who conducts community healing rites, the drum circle leader or facilitator must hold sacred space and guide the pattern, flow, and energy of the drumming toward the ritual's intended goal. Even in trance states, a skilled facilitator maintains a portion of conscious awareness in order to stay in tune with the pulse of the circle.

Shamanic drum circles are an effective way to restore the web of life. The drums shape available energy into a powerful vortex that spirals out into the resonating circle of life. The true power of a shamanic circle comes from the capacity of its members to work together for a common goal. When they are of one heart, of one mind and of one accord, a circle of shamanic practitioners can effectively heal individuals, communities and beyond. To learn more, read my *Shamanic Drumming Circles Guide.*[8]

Going deeper

Shamanic drumming is a meaningful practice that deepens our connection to spirit. Drumming, by its very nature, creates rhythms that carry us very quickly into deeper levels of consciousness. The deeper we go in our relationship with spirit, the closer we get to what we need. To go deeper and become more effective, we can use intentionality in our spiritual practice. Intention can be aligned with process rather than with a specific outcome. By setting the intention to go deeper, uncover more, and expand our capacity to create the results we desire, we can truly harness the power of drumming.

10 good reasons to harness the power of drumming

1. To induce natural altered states of consciousness: Researchers have found that if a drum beat frequency of around three to four beats per second is sustained for at least fifteen minutes, it will induce significant altered states in most people, even on their first attempt. This ease of induction of altered states contrasts dramatically with the months or years of practice usually required by most meditative disciplines to induce significant effects. Rhythmic stimulation is a simple and effective technique for affecting states of mind.
2. To ground you in the present moment: Drumming helps alleviate stress that is created from holding on to the past or worrying about the future. When one plays a drum, one is placed squarely in the here and now. The drumbeat somehow manages to anchor you while simultaneously creating a sensation of movement. Another paradox of rhythm is that it has both the capacity to move your awareness out of your body into realms beyond time and space and to ground you firmly in the present moment. It allows you to maintain a portion of ordinary awareness while experiencing non-ordinary awareness. This permits full recall later of the visionary experience.
3. To become a vessel of healing: When you drum, close your eyes and focus your attention on the sound of the drum. Become one with the beat of the drum. Allow the drum to empty your mind of all but the rhythm you are playing. You must empty yourself to be filled up by the healing power of the divine. Emptiness is the true nature of reality and the goal of all meditative practice. When you get out of your own way to allow spirit to work through you, you become a vessel of healing for others.
4. To release negative feelings and emotional trauma: Drumming can help people express and address their emotional issues. Unexpressed

feelings and emotions can form energy blockages. The physical stimulation of drumming removes blockages and produces emotional release. Sound vibrations resonate through every cell in the body, stimulating the release of negative cellular memories. As a substance abuse counselor and musician working with at-risk youth, Ed Mikenas finds that, "Drumming emphasizes self-expression, teaches how to rebuild emotional health, and addresses issues of violence and conflict through expression and integration of emotions."[9]

5. To reduce tension, anxiety and stress: Drumming induces deep relaxation, lowers blood pressure and reduces stress. Stress, according to current medical research, contributes to nearly all disease and is a primary cause of such life-threatening illnesses as heart attacks, strokes and immune system breakdowns. A groundbreaking 2005 study demonstrated that drumming not only reduces stress, but reverses genetic switches that turn on the stress response believed responsible in the development of common diseases.

6. To create sacred space: The drum is also a versatile instrument for creating sacred space. You can use it to summon the spirits into a ritual or ceremony. According to Wallace Black Elk, the renowned Lakota spiritual leader, "When you pray with that drum, when the spirits hear that drum, it echoes. They hear this drum, and they hear your voice loud and clear."[10] Conversely, a forceful beat of the drum can be used to drive away malevolent spirits or intrusive energies that cause confusion, disease and disharmony. Used in this way, the drum facilitates the creation of a purified sacred space.

7. To gain insight into a question or situation: You can take concerns into a drum meditation in order to access personal revelation from within. The essence of mindful drumming is the experience of direct revelation, which comes through as a feeling, impression or intuition. Drumming stills the mind's internal dialogue, allowing you to view life and life's problems from a detached, spiritual perspective not easily achieved in a state of ordinary consciousness.

8. To build community through drum circles: In a society in which traditional family and community-based systems of support have become increasingly fragmented, drum circles provide a sense of connectedness with others and interpersonal support. A drum circle provides an opportunity to connect with your own spirit at a deeper level, and also to connect with a group of other like-minded people. Shamanic circles

provide an authentic experience of unity and interconnectedness. Group drumming alleviates self-centeredness, isolation and alienation.

9. To access a higher power: Recent studies demonstrate that the drumming provides a secular approach to accessing a higher power and applying spiritual perspectives. According to research published in the *American Journal of Public Health*, "shamanic drumming directly supports the introduction of spiritual factors found significant in the healing process. Shamanic activities bring people efficiently and directly into immediate encounters with spiritual forces, focusing the client on the whole body and integrating healing at physical and spiritual levels. This process allows them to connect with the power of the universe, to externalize their own knowledge, and to internalize their answers; it also enhances their sense of empowerment and responsibility. These experiences are healing, bringing the restorative powers of nature to clinical settings."[11]

10. To achieve self-realization: Drumming facilitates the realization or fulfillment of one's own potential. As Ute-Tiwa holy man Joseph Rael points out in his book, *Being and Vibration*, "Drumming opens up three basic vibrations. Drumming awakens the self. Drumming heightens the ability of perception, and drumming enables the person to see into the deeper realms of the self."[12] Drumming connects us to our true self—to our soul. Once connected to our soul, we can discover and actualize our true potential.

THE GREAT SHIFT

Chapter 4

Divining the Way to Harmony

To know harmony is to know the eternal. To know the eternal is to know enlightenment.
—Lao Tzu, author of the Tao Te Ching and founder of Taoism[1]

Divination is the art of gaining insight into a question or situation by the interpretation of signs or omens. The goal of shamanic divination is to encourage well-being by helping a person live in harmony with the universe around them. One of the best known systems of divination is the I Ching, or Book of Changes. For some 3,000 years, people have turned to the I Ching to help them uncover the meaning of their experience and to bring their actions into harmony with their underlying purpose. Consulting the I Ching is one of the best ways I know of to restore harmony wherever there is disharmony. Restoring harmony is the primary work of the shaman.

The I Ching emerged in China as a fortune-telling guide. According to legend, it was Fu Hsi, the first emperor of China, who originated the linear yin/yang system of the I Ching. He discovered the symbols in the pattern of markings on the shell of a turtle that emerged from a river. It began with eight three-lined symbols called trigrams, which represented all of the fundamental phenomena in the universe. When doubled, the eight trigrams became sixty-four six-lined hexagrams. This doubling process produced trigram relationships, such as "Heaven and Earth unite," the symbolic elements of the hexagram for "Peace." The underlying idea of the I Ching is that the sixty-four hexagrams represent the basic circumstances of change in the universe. When you consult the I Ching, it responds in the form of a hexagram (or hexagrams if there are changing lines) that provides guidance for your specific circumstance at the moment.[2]

Otherwise known as the Classic of Changes, this archaic and enigmatic text was the fountainhead of Taoist and Confucian thought. Its philosophy encompasses such issues as ethics, social values and personal responsibility. It conveys archetypal paradigms and perspectives that serve as models of ethical and harmonious living. Over time, the symbolism of the I Ching was interpreted in commentaries by thousands of Confucian, Taoist, and

Buddhist adepts, inspiring a renaissance in philosophy, religion, art, literature, science and medicine throughout East Asia, and eventually the West. In short, the I Ching became, in the words of a nineteenth-century Chinese commentator, "the mirror of men's minds."[3]

The wisdom unveiled in the I Ching is simple and consistent: if we relate correctly, keeping ourselves in harmony with the universe, all things work out beneficially for all concerned. The I Ching reflects the philosophy that all events (past, present and future) are part of a single, interrelated whole. It describes the universe as a vast, singular entity in which all things are in continuous cyclical change. The central theme is that all things move in predictable patterns or cycles, therefore no situation is static or immutable.

The original text of the I Ching was organized by King Wen of Zhou around 1150 BC and remains virtually unchanged to the present. It consists of sixty-four hexagrams or six-line symbols which consist of upper and lower trigrams. King Wen is credited with having stacked the eight trigrams in their various permutations to create the sixty-four hexagrams. He is also said to have written the judgments which are appended to each hexagram. Each hexagram is accompanied by a text containing folk poetry, historical tales and commentary. These ancient writings describe the conditions associated with the sixty-four archetypal patterns of cyclical change. They convey the laws and principles pertaining to time and change. The hexagram symbols reveal the patterns through which change manifests itself in the ebb and flow of time. According to renowned I Ching scholar Richard Wilhelm, "The hexagrams and lines in their movements and changes mysteriously reproduced the movements and changes of the macrocosm."[4]

The I Ching is a codebook of archetypal patterns in which the hexagrams counsel appropriate action in the moment for a given set of circumstances. Each moment has a pattern to it, and everything that happens in that moment is interconnected. Based on the synchronicity of the universe and the laws of probability, the I Ching responds to an inquiry in the form of a hexagram. By evaluating the hexagram that describes your current pattern of relationship, you can divine the outcome and act accordingly. The oracle serves as a gauge—a precise means for placing oneself in relation to the pattern or way of cyclical change, and that way is known as Tao (the absolute principle underlying the universe).

The I Ching is a microcosm of all possible human situations. It serves as a dynamic map, whose function is to reveal one's relative position in the cosmos of events. The hexagram texts address the sixty-four archetypal human situations. The commentary of each hexagram reveals the optimal strategy for integrating or harmonizing with the inevitable for a given condition. It provides the appropriate response to your inquiry. It affords a holistic perspective of your current condition and discusses the proper or correct way to address the situation.

The rhythm archetypes

The I Ching is the wellspring of Chinese thought, stressing the connection between humanity's destiny and the natural world. Philosophically, it describes the Tao, or universe, as a single, flowing, rhythmic being, and all things in it in constant cyclical change. The eternal Tao continuously gives birth to the one universal energy, which expresses itself as two polar but co-creative aspects, yin and yang. The sages of ancient China revealed the most profound secret of the universe—that yin and yang pulsate within all things, and in unison they are the moving force of nature and all its manifestations. The ebb and flow of yin and yang create the cycles and rhythms of life.

By contemplating nature, the wise sages perceived all of the rhythms and energy patterns that arise from the interaction of yin and yang. By observing patterns of events arising in the natural world, the social world and the inner world of the psyche, they deciphered nature's rhythmic code. They then coded these rhythmic patterns into a "book of life." The I Ching's sixty-four hexagrams represent a code or program of the operating principle of life itself. Each six-lined symbol is the visual representation of a rhythm archetype. The rhythm archetypes are the "sonic seeds" of all that exists.

The entire universe is created through vibration and can be influenced through vibration. T'an Ch'iao, a Taoist adept of the tenth century, expressed this potential when he wrote, "When energy moves, sound is emitted; when sound comes forth, energy vibrates. When energy vibrates, influences are activated and things change. Therefore it is possible thereby to command wind and clouds, produce frost and hail, cause phoenixes to sing, get bears to dance, make friends with spiritual luminescences."[5]

The hexagram rhythms

Moreover, each six-lined symbol depicts a particular drum pattern, which renders the essence of each hexagram into sound. A solid yang line _____ represents one whole beat, while a broken yin line __ __ represents two half beats or a heartbeat. For example, the rhythmic pattern of Hexagram 58, "The Joyous," resembles the opening beats of the familiar processional "The Wedding March." This simple drum pattern is depicted below. Please note that the hexagrams are read from bottom to top.

Line 6	__ __	drum—drum	in white
Line 5	_____	drum	dressed
Line 4	_____	drum	all
Line 3	__ __	drum—drum	the bride
Line 2	_____	drum	comes
Line 1	_____	drum	Here

Drumming is an innovative way to engage with an I Ching reading. This method was developed by Melinda "Mo" Maxfield in her book *Drumming the I Ching*.[6] It is a type of focus meditation, requiring total concentration. Drum meditation is a way to access the archetypal wisdom contained in each hexagram. As a form of meditation, drumming activates perceptions that can be attained by no other means. By drumming the hexagrams, one can achieve a level of intuitive understanding beyond linguistic interpretations. Archetypal knowledge is symbolic and non-linear. It does not lend itself readily to logical or verbal expression. It is wisdom that can only be experienced intuitively. The process is an effective meditative technique for self-exploration.

Consulting the I Ching

If you do not have a copy of the I Ching, you can easily consult the oracle online. There are many websites that offer a free I Ching reading.[7] To consult the I Ching, one must first frame an inquiry. Formulating an appropriate question and writing it down is a key element in the process of divination. Focusing on a question develops a receptive state of mind and helps you clarify what it is you are truly seeking. It is important to word your inquiry in a concise and clear-cut manner. A vague question will elicit an ambiguous or misleading response. Appropriate inquiries might be worded as follows:

1. "Which hexagram(s) am I to work with today?"
2. "Which hexagram(s) best describes my current situation?"
3. "Which hexagram(s) is most relevant to my current predicament?"
4. "Which hexagram(s) should I drum at this time to heal my illness?"
5. "Which hexagram(s) should I drum at this time to attune to the Tao?"

Interpreting the message

The I Ching does not answer a question in a direct, logical manner. It responds in the form of a hexagram that serves as a model or paradigm of appropriate behavior. It provides the framework within which to perceive and comprehend the archetypal condition related to your query. It provides a holistic perspective and comments on the situation or condition. It offers suggestions on the best way to approach this condition. It presents advice for what to do to act in accord with or avoid a particular prediction. You must then interpret the message and determine for yourself the most appropriate course of action with regard to your inquiry. This process engages the subjective and intuitive mind.

When your interpretation differs from the eventual outcome, then reevaluate the commentary in light of what actually transpired. In this way, you develop proficiency in your ability to interpret the I Ching's sometimes paradoxical and enigmatic aphorisms. At times, the oracle will provide an incomprehensible response that does not seem to fit the question posed. When this occurs, the I Ching may be overriding your stated inquiry in order to address a more significant issue, an unstated concern, or unconscious projection. The oracle may also be alerting you to an impending crisis or significant change. Keep in mind that all conditions are transitory. Nothing is permanently fixed, so whether you like or dislike the response, conditions will eventually change with regard to your inquiry.

Drumming the hexagram

As the alphabet encodes a language, providing channels of communication, so each hexagram symbol contains the potential of communication and understanding. The hexagrams are resonant structures that convey ideas, words and energy. Resonance is the key to unlocking the rhythm generating patterns of the I Ching code. As Chang Yeh-Yuan, a Taoist monk of the fifth century observed, "The fundamental idea of the I Ching can be expressed in one single word: Resonance."[8] Resonance is the ability of a sound wave to impart its energy to a substance such as air, wood, metal, or the human body, making it vibrate in sympathy. This sympathetic resonance implies an exchange of energy and consciousness between two things.

By drumming a hexagram rhythm, it is possible to create a resonant field of communication. Remember that each hexagram is read from bottom to top. While drumming a hexagram, you should have a receptive attitude of calm, positive expectation. Such resonant receptivity allows whatever factors or forces are present to fully penetrate your senses. Any attempt to analyze the experience will only disrupt the resonant field, obstructing your connection. Follow your inner sense of timing as to both the tempo and time span to drum. Trust your internal timing. It connects you to the resonances affecting your situation. The key is to still the mind, and focus your attention on the hexagram image.

As the drumming progresses and your inner image of the hexagram becomes clearer, close your eyes and feel yourself being carried away by the rhythm, as if going on a journey into yourself. With time and patience, the rhythm archetype will begin to release a rush of intuitive ideas. Inspiration and insight regarding the situation may flow into your awareness. However, it is not essential that you become consciously aware of any particular insight or guidance. Simply resonate in sync with the vibrational pattern that collectively reflects your current condition or connection to Tao.

After drumming the hexagram, repose in the sonic afterglow. After the final drum beat fades away, an inaudible, yet perceptible pulsation persists for a brief period. You can feel this silent pulse resonating throughout your body. You can sense every particle in your body pulsing in sympathy with the rhythm you just played. This synchrony of inner pulse with the appropriate hexagram rhythm brings you into accord with the conditions and forces governing or affecting your inquiry.

It is not necessary to drum the hexagram every time you consult the I Ching. Not every inquiry, after all, addresses an important issue or concern. The best recommendation is to begin by consulting and drumming the I Ching regularly and informally in order to become familiar and comfortable with the process. Casting, interpreting and drumming a hexagram on a regular basis develops the intuitive and subjective aspects of consciousness. As you cultivate these qualities, you expand your awareness, enhance your understanding, and enrich your life experiences. You learn the appropriate way to respond in any situation. Such synchronous behavior brings you into accord with the dynamics of change.

Synchronicity

Carl Jung, the eminent psychologist, defined synchronicity as "meaningful coincidence," one that involves an internal psychological event that corresponds to an external observable event. The I Ching is based on the principle of meaningful coincidences, or the synchronicity of the universe. This is the proposition that the human experience is a microcosm and reflection of universal law and order. Humanity is the universe, occurring in every moment. Each human being is a hologram of the Cosmos, a weaving together of universal information from a particular point of view. As American author and human potentialist George Leonard put it: "Each human being consists of pure information expressed as rhythmic waves that start as infinitesimal vibrations of subatomic particles and build outward as ever-widening resonant hierarchies of atoms, molecules, cells, organs, organisms, families, bands, tribes, nations, civilizations, and beyond."[9] At every phase of unfoldment, every entity is interwoven through the resonant web of information that is the universe.

Synchronicity relates the individual to the totality. Synchronicity attunes us to the flow of a unified, harmonious universe in which everything is interconnected and interdependent. Synchronicity is the underlying basis of the I Ching. It teaches principles through which one may live in harmony with and experience oneness with the Tao. We live in a world of harmony, perfect rhythm. Disrhythm and discord arise only when we create limitations on our capacity to resonate totally and completely with the eternal rhythm of Tao.

The Tao of drumming

Tao is the most comprehensive concept in Chinese culture, the center of all philosophical and spiritual belief. It may be defined as a path, a way, a doctrine, or the natural process of the universe itself. Every art and science is called a Tao, or a way. From a rhythmic perspective, the I Ching offers and represents a Tao (or way) of drumming. It is a way to harmony and balance, and the drum is the instrument of attunement. Through a knowing use of the hexagram rhythms, we can drum ourselves into perfect octaves of attunement and accord with the universe.

Our situation in the cosmos of events

Before writing this book, I consulted the I Ching in order to gain some insight into the dire situation of our world today. When I consulted the I Ching regarding our current situation on the planet, I received Hexagram 36, "Darkening of the Light." This hexagram symbolizes the sun sinking into the earth and is often associated with the "dark night of the soul." It denotes a time of darkness when oppressive forces obscure the beauty and clarity of light. The commentary of Hexagram 36 states, "Here a man of dark nature is in a position of authority and brings harm to the wise and able man."[10] It is a time of maximum darkness and ignorance; a time when the dark forces of the unconscious are at their peak.

According to the I Ching, when the darkness of stupidity reigns in human affairs, it is best that you keep your brilliance "hidden under a bushel basket." The oracle counsels us to show our intelligence by concealing it. Lao Tzu, the great philosopher of Taoism, gives us the best paraphrase of the idea in a famous proverb from his classic, the Tao Te Ching: "Those who know do not speak. Those who speak do not know."[11] In dealing with the masses, true leaders act unobtrusively while in fact being illuminated. What sages learn is to quietly become more illuminated each day unnoticed by others.

For the time being, it is in our best interests to accept the situation. Like the time of winter, the situation requires that we turn within to stoke our inner fire with spiritual practice. A spiritual practice is something you do every single day that grounds you in your own truth by connecting you with your essential self. So we must tend to our inner light and maintain a low profile. As long as we conceal our inner glow, it cannot be extinguished. Until conditions are more favorable, remain yielding and compliant externally, while maintaining your inner vision, convictions and principles. Such an attitude will sustain your inner light in even the darkest of times. Try not to become too depressed or anxious; this period will pass. The darkness that is now manifesting within humanity will eventually consume itself and perish, for it has no inner light to sustain it. The sun will rise again.

10 good reasons to consult the I Ching

1. To foresee or foretell future events: The I Ching unveils the philosophy that all events (past, present and future) are part of a single, interrelated whole. The future develops out of the present according to a set of fixed laws. To know the present, then, is to know the future.
2. To discover hidden knowledge: We can consult the I Ching to discover knowledge buried within the subconscious. Casting a hexagram was devised in ancient China as a mechanism for reflecting or mirroring what the subconscious or inner self already knows. The subconscious mind knows which hexagram best describes our current situation or condition. It knows because it accesses the sum of consciousness immanent in all phenomena. The subconscious mind is able to gather the information desired and influence the casting to indicate the most appropriate hexagram.
3. To bring the essential self into accord with the Cosmos: The central idea of the I Ching is that divination is a means of coming into harmony with the ultimate reality of the universe. We can use the oracle to divine the way to harmony with the Tao. It is a pathway to the infinite Tao, the unknowable force that guides the universe and everything in it. If we relate correctly, keeping ourselves in tune with the Cosmos, all things work out favorably for all concerned.
4. To explore and develop the inner self: More than an oracle, the I Ching is a symbolic blueprint or map of reality. It is an extraordinary symbol system that represents the fundamental aspects of our physical, mental and spiritual experience. The hexagram images of the I Ching are semiotic. They are resonant structures that convey ideas, information and energy. As symbols, the linear images convey paradoxical truths regarding the nature of existence in an intuitive, nonlinear manner. They provide a means of exploring and developing the innermost self.
5. To effect or harmonize with change: As a counsel and advisor, the I Ching reveals the optimal manner for integrating or harmonizing with the inevitable for any given condition. On the other hand, fate is not entirely predetermined. In his invaluable translation of the I

Ching, Richard Wilhelm states, "...fate can be shaped if its laws are known. The reason why we can oppose fate is that reality is always conditioned, and these conditions of time and space limit and determine it. The spirit, however, is not bound by these determinants and can bring them about as its own purposes require."[12] We have free will; therefore we can change fate.

6. To connect with our inner truth: Inner truth reflects, like a mirror, the higher, universal truth that exists in every situation. If we rely on the truth of our inner voice to guide us, we can readily adapt and flow with the shifting currents of change. Flowing water is the image of Tao and shows us the way to unimpeded harmony. Water flows continually and effortlessly to its destination and never loses its essential nature despite the obstacles it encounters. Like water, we should remain constant in our virtue and flow over and around any obstacles in our path. In every situation, we should outwardly go with the flow while inwardly adhering to our inner truth, to our sense of what is correct.

7. To develop the intuitive and subjective mind: Casting and interpreting a hexagram on a regular basis develops the intuitive and subjective aspects of consciousness. These qualities of mind are an amazing source of creative power, wisdom and understanding. They transcend the realms of experience or reasoning. As we cultivate these qualities, we expand our awareness, enhance our understanding, and enrich our life experiences.

8. To ground us in the present moment: As a system of divination, the I Ching reflects our current connection with Tao. It serves to freeze the present moment at the time of our inquiry, responding in the form of a hexagram. It affords a holistic perspective of our current condition and discusses the proper or correct way to address the situation. In an age of ever-accelerating, sometimes bewildering change, working with the I Ching helps ground us in the moment and compels us to meditate on the words in the commentary.

9. To access the time-honored wisdom of the I Ching: The I Ching is a collection of practical wisdom, pertaining to every conceivable situation. The I Ching has been consulted through the ages, in both China and the West, for answers to fundamental questions about the world and our place in it. The wisdom of the I Ching reveals the universal

laws that govern us all, and shows us how to live in harmony with those laws to live a life of peace, love and prosperity.

10. To harmonize the cosmic and the terrestrial: Sustained by the Earth and transformed by the heavens, humanity is the bridge that unites the earthly (body), human (mind), and heavenly (spirit) realms. Through divination, we can bring the body, mind and spirit into accord. We can transform personal experience and influence the interactions of the three cosmic realms. It is our destiny to bring the three realms into accord. It is our fate to stand between heaven and Earth. When we resist our fate, we suffer. When we accept it, we are happy.

THE GREAT SHIFT

Chapter 5

Practicing the Art of Shapeshifting

Many of us are learning to utilize shapeshifting to transform the world's environmental state, with universal peace being a primary goal. From a shamanic perspective, shapeshifting begins with intent. Intent, energy, and action: Only when these three human forces are in place can you have true shapeshifting.
—John Perkins, American author, economist and environmentalist[1]

Shapeshifting is the shamanic art of shifting our old, entrenched thought patterns and perspectives in order to transform ourselves, both as individuals and communities. An important aspect of shapeshifting is the ability to transform or morph into a helping spirit. These helping spirits might be the spirits of nature, animals, plants, the elements, ancestors, gods, goddesses or teachers from various religious traditions. The purpose of shapeshifting is to adopt the perspective of a helping spirit in order to see the world through their eyes and to develop a personal relationship. The reason for developing personal relationships with spirit helpers is to gain wisdom, healing techniques and other vital information that can benefit the community.

Whether you realize it or not, you have always had helping spirits. Helping spirits are like family and friends, and each has a unique personality. One of the things I have learned working with spirits is that they often prompt me, through urges, to do one thing or another. This is a common form of communication and instruction by helping spirits. Some shamans compare the spirits to radio waves. Spirits can travel on radio waves, phone lines, or cell phones. Basically, a spirit helper is a coherent energy pattern that can take form as an animal, plant, ancestor, deity, element or even a mythical creature such as a unicorn or dragon.

Mythical creatures manifest in our conscious, mythic awareness because they still exist in the world of archetypes that underlies our reality. The same holds true for creatures that lived in the past and that are now extinct. A group archetype or oversoul of each extinct species continues to exist in the unseen world, so a person may have a dinosaur or mammoth as a power animal.

All helping spirits are extensions of the one spirit that pervades all existence, whom we could call the Creator, Tao or Great Mystery. Spirits are a natural manifestation of human consciousness. They manifest in two main categories: those who have physical form and those who do not or no longer do. Those helping spirits that have a physical form are known as elementals and may include representatives of the plant, animal, or mineral kingdoms, or an element such as air, water, fire, earth, sun, moon, planets, stars, and so on.

Spirit helpers that do not operate out of the physical realm may include ancestors who choose to be of service to us or divine archetypes such as angels and devas. In the cultures of the past, these typically were the gods and goddesses of mythology. These helping spirits can take on a human form temporarily and act as intermediaries between us and the powers of the universe. They may include great spiritual teachers such as Jesus, Buddha, Lao Tzu, and so on.

Trees and plants also manifest as helping spirits. Plant spirits are one of the major allies of shamans for healing, seeing, dreaming and empowerment. Shamans heal using their knowledge of plant spirits as well as the plant's medicinal properties. When the shaman does not know what plant medicine to use for a sick person, the plant spirit tells him. Plants, however, are more than their chemical components. They are intelligent beings that have the capacity to raise consciousness to a level where true healing can take place. Plants have always evolved before their animal counterparts and offer profound guidance regarding our own spiritual evolution.

Power animals

The majority of helping spirits take animal forms called power animals. Power animals are also called guardian spirits, spirit allies, totem animals and tutelary animals. A power animal is the archetypal oversoul that represents the entire species of that animal. It is actually the spirit of one of the "first people," as they are called, who at the end of mythic times turned into the animals as we know them today.

In the worldview of the shaman, power animals or animal archetypes such as Eagle, Coyote and Bear represent and protect their entire species. When you connect with a power animal, you align yourself with the collective strength and wisdom of the entire species. One of the most important gifts that animal allies offer is protection and guardianship to the shaman during arduous shamanic tasks. Without this alliance, it is widely accepted that it is impossible to become a shaman.

Power animals are themselves great teachers and shamans. In many shamanic cultures, the knowledge imparted by a power animal is considered more important than the practical guidance of a master shaman. Power animals are valuable allies who can help you navigate through life's challenges and transitions. Many animals will come to guide you, some briefly and others throughout your life. One has as many power animals as volunteer themselves. We also discover through relationship with them that the animal spirits may have very individual and specific teachings for each of us. Similar to the way friendships develop gradually, our relationships with power animals grow and deepen based on repeated interaction and building trust over time.

Power animals offer humans a much needed medicine. They remind us of what is innocent and truthful. Animals subsist from the heart, with a deep instinctual knowing that is always connected to the web of life. They live from the heart and are not entrapped by their reason. Humans, on the other hand, tend to live from the head, trying to figure everything out. But the energy that comes in from the source is directed through our hearts. We come into our own power when we learn to live from the heart. The heart attunes us to the flow of a complex, ever-changing universe.

The magic of shapeshifting

One of the best ways to connect with power animals is through the art of shapeshifting. In the shaman's world, animals are kin, an ancient belief reflected in mythology and in animism—the belief that non-human entities are sentient, spiritual beings. It is a mental world where the seen and the unseen, the material and the spiritual merge. As their helping spirits, the shamans "might use animals, anything that grows," says Osuitok Ipeelee, an esteemed Arctic Inuit sculptor. "It was well known that the animals the shamans controlled had the ability to turn into humans. When a shaman was using his magic he had a real change of personality. When the animals entered into him he'd be chanting loudly; if a shaman was turning into a certain animal, he'd make that animal sound. Once he was filled inside, he'd begin to change; his face and his skin followed."[2]

THE GREAT SHIFT

Shapeshifting is more than just transforming into an animal as is often depicted in shamanic accounts and tales. It is the ability to shift your energies to adapt to the demands and changes of daily life. We all learn which activities, behaviors and attitudes support or hinder our survival and growth. It is a natural and instinctual ability that we all share. The minimal development of this talent is the ability to mimic. We often mimic for the purpose of learning something or to blend in with our social or physical environment. It implies changing one's appearance or behavior rather than just using what you already have. Actors, for example, are known for their ability to take on the characteristics of another person or thing. Physically mimicking the appearance and behavior of an animal will help you to shapeshift into that animal.

The magic of shapeshifting can be understood as the ability to fully adopt the perspective of a spirit animal in order to understand and share their feelings. Through the process of inviting an animal spirit into your body and consciousness, you change your understanding of the world. Shapeshifting into an animal is not a practice to be taken lightly, and one should not attempt it unless they have a comprehensive understanding of grounding techniques. Depending on the animal and the person involved, it can be difficult to completely rid the self of the animal spirit, and this can be a problem if the animal's attributes are quite different from your personality and/or you find it becoming negative or unhelpful.

Shapeshifting is a technique of changing from one energetic state to another. It is based on the belief that everything is made of energy and that we are all connected through this source energy. A shapeshifter is one who manipulates their energy or aura to access a higher or inner power in order to grow and learn. The human aura is the energy field that surrounds the human body in all directions. All shapeshifting occurs on an energy level. If everything is broadcasting its own energy pattern and if you could match and rebroadcast the same pattern, then you would take on the appearance and qualities of the thing you were matching. The only constraining factor is the degree of belief, connection and energy. To experience this for yourself, try the following simple exercise:

1. Create and open sacred space as you would for other spiritual work, dim the lights, and sit comfortably erect in a chair or on the floor.
2. Ground yourself with some mindful breathing. Close your eyes and focus on your breath until you are calm and relaxed.

3. Call upon an animal that you have an affinity with. Visualize and invite this animal spirit to come into your body and consciousness.
4. Meditate with it. Be open to the feelings and sensations of being that animal. It is not uncommon to be and see the animal at the same time.
5. Simply observe whatever happens for a few minutes, and then thank the spirit animal and release it.

Shapeshifting to any degree will help you develop a kinship with your animal relatives. Learning to shift your awareness opens your heart and mind to the wisdom and strength of the animal world. You must empty yourself so that spirit can embody you. "Become like a hollow bone," Oglala Lakota elder and Heyoka clown Don Dream Seeker Fasthorse once advised me in the sweat lodge.[3]

Power animal drumming

Drumming is an excellent way to induce embodiment trance states and facilitate shapeshifting. The shaman uses embodiment trance to bring a helping spirit into his or her physical body to better use and/or learn from the spirit energy. When an animal spirit is invoked, there is often an accompanying rhythm that comes through. Shamans frequently use these unique rhythms to summon their helping spirits for the work at hand. As Ted Andrews explains in his book *Animal Speak*, "Some are so skilled at drumming, they can duplicate the rhythms of various animals. There is snake drumming, wolf drumming, hawk drumming—a drumming for every animal. As the rhythm is created it plays upon the metabolism of the individual causing entrainment—the individual's own heart and metabolic rhythm is brought into synchronization with the drum beat. This is used to facilitate a shapeshifting, an aligning with the archetypal forces represented by the animal."[4]

Through drumming, it is possible to invoke and embody power animal archetypes. I have a repertoire of spirit calling rhythms that I recorded on an album titled *Power Animal Drumming*.[5] The rhythms on this recording evolved over many years through me and fellow shamanic practitioners who gained and nurtured enduring personal relationships with helping animal spirits. Each drum pattern creates a vibratory resonance that allows these spirit helpers to be called forth. Each rhythm transmits a supportive resonance or sound pattern to which the body can attune. As the rhythm invokes the intended spirit, the drummer comes into resonance with this spirit helper as well, resulting in an exchange of perspective, energy and awareness. To experience this for yourself, try the following exercise for shapeshifting into an eagle:

1. First, do some preliminary research on the eagle, its habits and behaviors. Become familiar enough with it to be able to clearly visualize it in your mind.

2. When you are ready, create a purified sacred space as you would for other spiritual work. After preparing sacred space, you should ritually open the space by calling in the spiritual energies of the seven directions: East, South, West, North, Up, Down and Within. Call out to your helping spirits for help and protection. Dim the lights and sit comfortably erect in a chair or on the floor. Close your eyes and center and ground yourself with some mindful breathing.

3. The next step is to frame a simple and clear statement of your intentions. Whether asking for help or merely getting acquainted with an animal, one must clearly convey the purpose of invoking them.

4. After clearly stating your intention, begin drumming the slow, steady metronome-like rhythm of the eagle-beat, and then gradually build in intensity to a tempo of four to seven beats per second. The ascending tempo will induce a deep embodiment trance state and facilitate the shapeshifting.

5. As the drumming progresses, vividly imagine with every sense an eagle in front of you. This specific imagery serves as an invitation, literally drawing the animal to you. Mentally review all of its qualities. Eagle symbolizes vision, clarity and foresight. Eagle is known for its ability to help us open our soul to spirit quests and to soar to great spiritual heights.

6. Now imagine that your body is merging with that of the eagle. Visualize the energy of the eagle awakening within you, along with all of its corresponding abilities. You may feel it, see it, sense it or simply imagine it. As you focus on it, it will occur. All energy follows thought, and Eagle rules the realm of thought. Allow the change to come slowly. It is not uncommon to be and see the animal simultaneously. Be open to the sensations and feelings of being that animal. Feeling is the most important sensation because you want to imagine what it feels like to be that animal. It helps to mimic the posture,

movements and sounds of the animal you are invoking. The degree of merging is limited by any negative attitudes such as reluctance or doubt. The goal is to merge to the greatest degree possible while still retaining a bit of self-awareness.

7. Finally, separate from the animal by imagining yourself back in your body. Do not rush the transformation. Imagine the animal fully and completely outside of you once more. Thank the animal for its power, presence and assistance. Then allow its image to dissipate.

Be flexible in the above steps. Adapt and experiment with them. Shapeshifting is an expressive art. For it to become truly magical, you must employ your own creative imagination and intuition. This exercise is only a beginning. It will not make you a master shapeshifter. To become a good shapeshifter, you must master the art of observation. You cannot shapeshift into an animal if you do not know its behavior, movements and characteristics. Begin by watching an animal's behavior and record your observations, your feelings and your insights. Mimic its postures, movements and sounds. Imagine what it would be like to be that animal.

By following the steps outlined in the preceding exercise, you can practice shapeshifting into any power animal you feel an affinity with. When you transform into an animal, you embody its qualities and abilities. A merging of energy and consciousness occurs. Power animals have much to share if you listen with your heart. They may teach you some special ways you can use the drum for your shamanic work that you did not know before. They may teach you a rhythm for invoking and enlivening it. Shapeshifting will help you develop a kinship with your animal relatives and the ability to invoke their power for the benefit of the community. Keep in mind that animal spirits choose to come into relationship with the person seeking. You can seek power animals, but the spirits must choose. I have seen people seek power animals yet never get chosen.

Shapeshifting is not without its risks. As mentioned earlier, it is good to have a comprehensive knowledge of grounding before attempting shapeshifting. Otherwise it can sometimes be quite difficult to fully ground yourself into your body and restore self-awareness. Some power animals are tricksters, like coyote and crow, and I do not recommend working with them unless you are experienced with both shapeshifting and tricksters. Bear in mind that you should always be respectful of spirit animals, for we are all related. Remember to thank power animals, and seek practical ways to give something of value back to the animal world.

Spirit Horse

I strongly recommend that you build a relationship with the spirit of Horse through prayer and invocation. You can call upon Spirit Horse to merge with you in shapeshifting. If you ask, Horse may even take you on a shamanic journey. As a spirit guide, Horse is a messenger to and from the spirit world and a psychopomp who leads departed souls into the afterlife. Horse represents personal power, stamina, endurance, freedom, independence, travel, adventure, and soul flight. According to American shaman Nicholas Noble Wolf, "Horse is a medicine or you could say a relationship with the spirit of Horse such that the Horse will let you (your spirit) ride him and will take you where you want to go."[6] Do you need to get somewhere physical or spiritual? Horse will assist you and serve as your guardian spirit, giving safety in your physical and metaphysical journeys.

Shapeshifting the world

Shapeshifting is about changing from one energetic state to another. Shapeshifting occurs on two different levels. The first level is personal, such as when an individual shifts their energy to match that of an animal or helping spirit. The purpose of personal shapeshifting is to take on the perspective of a helping spirit in order to see the world through their eyes and to build a mutually supportive relationship. The reason for building a relationship with a spirit helper is to acquire knowledge, wisdom, and a broader, deeper understanding of the world.

The second level of shapeshifting is social, such as when people collectively transform their organizations and communities. The purpose of social shapeshifting is to develop new thought and behavior patterns in order to change the social world. We can only change our social reality by changing the way we think—by changing our beliefs, expectations and assumptions which keep us stuck in a narrow perspective. Since all energy follows thought, shapeshifting is one of the most effective means of transforming societies. We create ourselves by how we invest this energy. What we focus our attention on is what our world becomes. By utilizing the principles of shapeshifting, we can transform our existing world into a sustainable, peaceful world where all our relations can thrive.

To bring about social change, we cannot fight who we are. We cannot beat the existing system; we have to build a better one instead. As American architect, systems theorist, and author R. Buckminster Fuller put it, "You never change things by fighting against the existing reality. To change something, build a new model that makes the old model obsolete."[7] We cannot change our political system by fighting it. We cannot change an oppressive government by voting for more progressive politicians. We cannot bring about the kind of social change we want by trying to tear down the parts of the old system that we do not like. We can only change the social structure by building a new model that is so desirable and so successful that people will clamor for it. From a shamanic perspective, we need to shapeshift a new world into being.

10 good reasons to practice the art of shapeshifting

1. To expand our perspectives and perceptions: Through shapeshifting, we can explore beyond the limits of human perspective and adopt the perspective of a helping spirit in order to see the world through their eyes. With all that is happening in the world today, it is good for us to get out of our own comfort zones in order to broaden our perspectives, to learn from and about others, to interact with the world differently, to see it with new eyes. By changing the way we perceive ourselves and the world around us, we shapeshift our reality.

2. To acquire wisdom and knowledge: Learning to shift your consciousness, to align with and adapt your energies to power animals, opens your heart and mind to the wisdom and healing knowledge of the animal realm. Our animal brothers and sisters have much to share if you listen with your heart. You can gain wisdom and insight into the deep relationships and patterns that exist among all things in the world.

3. To build relationship: A skillful shapeshifter works in sacred partnership with helping spirits—the animal spirits, the plant spirits and the nature spirits. Spirit helpers are the caretakers in the unseen world who want to support the Earth and her inhabitants at this time. They are here to teach us how to gather wisdom from the spiritual realms, the natural world, the past, the present and the future in order to give birth

to new ways of being. It is an alliance that fosters healing, problem solving and strong communities.

4. To embody a power animal's qualities and abilities: Shapeshifting into a spirit animal will help you manifest the attributes you desire from it. An exchange of energy and awareness takes place between you and the spirit you embody. Many animals will, when treated respectfully, bestow special gifts, powers or abilities to an individual. Some animals, like Lion, provide you with godly protection, looking for anything that will come into your home to cause harm. Aggressive animals, like Badger and Wolverine, can help you assert yourself positively. Nocturnal animals, like Owl, can help you see what is truly beneath the surface, what is hidden or in the shadows.

5. To facilitate reconciliation: Shapeshifting can be especially helpful in reconciling our differences with animals we do not like or fear. Contemplate what it means if you are not comfortable with a power animal. If you dislike or are afraid of an animal, it is especially important to connect with it and learn its wisdom. The message it holds for you will be particularly meaningful. Power animals help us connect to the parts of ourselves that we have lost or denied, so it may be mirroring a trait or quality that is ready to come back to help you be whole again.

6. To acquire protective powers: When we connect with a power animal, we align ourselves with the collective strength, power and archetypal energies of the entire species. Power animals empower and safeguard us when performing shamanic work. When in deep trance, they protect us from unwanted negative energies and intrusions. Power animals offer protection, guidance and assistance with a great many tasks beyond our personal abilities.

7. To navigate our rapidly changing world: We and the world around us are in a constant state of flux. Everything is constantly moving, changing and renewing. By practicing the art of shapeshifting, we learn how to shift from one energetic state to another to meet the demands and changes of daily life. We learn how to respond to life spontaneously, adapting to the shifting patterns of change. Through the art of shapeshifting, power animals become valuable allies who can help us navigate through life's challenges and transitions.

8. To feel and develop empathy toward our animal relatives: Empathy is the capacity to understand or feel what another being is experiencing from their perspective. It is the ability to exchange perspectives or to

"put oneself in another's shoes," so to speak. You try to imagine yourself in their place in order to understand what they are feeling or experiencing. Empathy is the tangible sense of our interconnectedness.

9. To support our spiritual quest for self-realization: Helping spirits, if engaged regularly and skillfully, offer flexibility, creativity and perseverance in fulfilling our own unique path. The spirits of nature are here to teach us to be better humans. They come to assist us in doing the principal unique thing we have come here to do in a way that benefits all living things.

10. To shapeshift a new world into being: According to many indigenous myths and legends, the present physical universe is the product of previous cycles of creation and destruction. For each stage of humanity's evolution there is created a corresponding development in the Earth. Each successive period of development concludes with catastrophic destruction to both Earth and humanity because humans misuse their creative powers for selfish purposes and forget their spiritual roles in the Creator's evolutionary plan. According to Mayan shaman Vieja Itza, "Each time it has been the Shapeshifter—what you might call sorcerer or prophet—who led us out of the abyss."[8] So fellow shapeshifters, I challenge you to lead the way in the Great Shift from old world to new.

THE GREAT SHIFT

Chapter 6

Taking the Shamanic Journey

What's really important about shamanism is that there is another reality that you can personally discover...we are not alone.
—Michael Harner, founder of The Foundation for Shamanic Studies[1]

Shamanism represents a universal conceptual framework found among indigenous tribal humans. It includes the belief that the natural world has two aspects: ordinary everyday awareness, formed by our behavior patterns, belief systems, social norms and cultural conditioning, and a second non-ordinary awareness accessed through altered states, or ecstatic trance, induced by shamanic practices such as repetitive drumming. The act of entering an ecstatic trance state is called the soul flight or shamanic journey, and it allows the practitioner to explore non-ordinary reality.

Shamanism is based on the principle that innate wisdom and guidance can be accessed through the inner senses in ecstatic trance. Basically, shamanic journeying is a way of communicating with your inner or true self and retrieving information. Your inner self is in constant communication with all aspects of your environment, seen and unseen. You need only journey within to find answers to your questions. You should have a question or objective in mind from the start. Shamanic journeying may be undertaken for purposes of divination, for personal healing, to meet one's power animal or spirit guide, or for any number of other reasons. After the journey, you must then interpret the meaning of your trance experience.

In shamanic terms, non-ordinary reality is more real than ordinary reality. When a journeyer enters non-ordinary reality, it is to obtain clarity and understanding about something in the everyday world that is not understood (e.g., Why am I sick? Why did this misfortune happen to me? How can I bring healing to myself and others? What is my mission and purpose in life?). Consequently, that is why journeying is sometimes called "going to the source." And that makes non-ordinary reality more authentic or real.

The drum, sometimes called the shaman's horse, provides a simple and effective way to induce ecstatic trance states. When a drum is played at an even tempo of three to four beats per second for at least fifteen minutes, most novices report that they can journey successfully even on their first attempt. The repetitive, rhythmic cadence of shamanic drumming is evocative of a horse on a journey. Siberian shamans describe it as the blissful, transcendent state that one mounts and rides from plane to plane. As Siberian shaman Tania Kobezhikova puts it, "My drum can connect me to the earth or carry me like a flying horse. Sometimes I send my spirits out, but other times I must go myself, alone or with the spirits."[2] During shamanic flight, the sound of the drum serves as a guidance system, indicating where the journeyer is at any moment or where they might need to go. The drumbeat also serves as a lifeline that the journeyer follows to return to their body and/or exit the trance state when the trance work is finished.

The shamanic journey is not a full out-of-body experience; the journeyer has a foot in both worlds. Part of the journeyer's consciousness is still lightly connected to the ordinary reality of the physical environment where they are located. This permits full recall later of the visionary experience, unlike the much deeper trance characteristic of embodiment trance or psychedelic drug-induced states. One maintains conscious control over the direction of travel, but does not know what mysteries will be uncovered. Transported by the driving beat of the drum, the journeyer travels to the inner planes of consciousness and back.

The shaman's universe

According to shamanic cosmology, there are three inner planes of consciousness: the Upper, Middle and Lower Worlds. There are numerous levels in both the Lower and Upper Worlds and they exist outside of time. The Upper or Celestial Realm is the home of the Star Nations and Thunder Beings; a related family of divine beings who bring about weather changes such as thunder, lightning, wind and rain. This shamanic realm relates to our higher self, or superconsciousness. It is the domain of divine archetypes such as angels, deities and evolved teachers. In this realm are the archetypal patterns or original energetic blueprints of everything that has or will ever exist. The Celestial Realm forms the matrix of possibilities that correspond to the world we experience through our mind and senses. All situations, conditions and states of being are a manifestation of a world of archetypes. Every event in the visible world is the effect of a "seed" image or pattern in the unseen world.

MICHAEL DRAKE

We can journey to the Upper World to acquire archetypal knowledge, to bring a vision into being, or to influence events in the material world. By interacting with the archetypes, we interact with their counterparts in the outer world. We can also go there for inspiration, insight, or to find ways to restore balance in the world. As anthropologist and author Felicitas Goodman points out, "One of the most pervasive traditions of shamanic cultures is the insight that there exists a patterned cosmological order, which can be disturbed by human activity."[3] When harmony between the human realm and the original intended pattern is disturbed, we can journey to the Celestial Realm to bring back the balance.

The Middle World is where spirit meets matter and is related to our ego or conscious self. The Middle World can be thought of as a non-ordinary mirror of ordinary reality. It is the spirit counterpart of the material realm and the inner region most like outer reality. The middle realm is so parallel to the world in which we live that a skilled journeyer can travel across it and visit all the places, people and things they know in ordinary reality. Spirit journeys in the Middle World provide a means of travel and communication without cars, planes or cell phones. It is a means of exploring our temporal landscape to find the location of healing herbs or lost objects, or to establish communication links over great distances.

To take a Middle World journey, simply imagine yourself walking out your front door and traveling through the landscape very quickly to look for something you have lost or to reach a distant destination. However, I do not recommend journeying to the Middle World unless you have a very good reason to go there. Unlike the upper and lower realms, where everything is guided by benevolence, the middle realm does not have benevolence or ethics at its core. That does not mean that it is a bad place. Rather, it is a place that mirrors what is happening in ordinary reality—the chaos of our times. It is a place full of risks and hidden dangers, such as holes in the ground that can entrap you. Traveling in this realm can be tricky even for an experienced journeyer. Moreover, the spirits who dwell in this realm cannot provide the wisdom, healing and empowerment you find in the Upper or Lower Worlds.

The Middle World is also populated with the souls of deceased persons who have not successfully crossed over to the other side. Middle World healing sometimes involves psychopomp work, the shamanic art of assisting deceased souls who have suffered traumatic deaths and remain earthbound. An earthbound soul is one who chooses not to "cross over" to the other side when their physical existence ends. When we die, there is usually a graceful transition into the afterlife. But when someone suffers a traumatic death such as murder, accident, war or suicide, they may not have an awareness of where and who they are. Other souls are held back by grieving relatives who cannot let them go. The purpose of funeral rites is to open the mourners to grief to unleash this powerful emotional energy and channel it in such a way that it will convey the newly deceased soul to the afterlife. If not channeled properly, grief is useless to the dead and dangerous to the living. Unfortunately, many of the psychopomp myths and rituals that once helped people prepare for this final rite of passage have become lost or forgotten.

Because so many souls are now trapped in the Middle World, many people are being called by spirit to become psychopomps. The psycho-pomp is a guide who leads the soul on its journey to the afterlife. The term derives from the Greek word *psuchopompos*, literally meaning the "guide of souls." The psychopomp is a universal, cross-cultural archetype. In Jungian psychology, the psychopomp is a mediator between the conscious and unconscious. It is symbolically personified in dreams as a wise man or woman, or often as an animal guide. Stories of psychopomps are wide-spread throughout the myths, legends and religious texts of cultures around the world. Psychopomps have been associated at different times and in different cultures with angels, horses, whip-poor-wills, ravens, dogs, crows and owls. In many cultures, the shaman also fulfills the role of the psychopomp. Their role is not to judge the deceased, but simply to provide safe passage.

The Lower World relates to our subconscious and unconscious mind. In Jungian psychology, it is also referred to as the realm of the personal shadow—the unwanted parts of our personality that we have repressed. This inner plane is the domain of animal spirits, spirit guides and the an-cestors; the place to which human spirits travel upon physical death. It is the realm of power animals, otherwise known as guardian spirits, totem animals and tutelary animals. A power animal is the archetypal oversoul that represents the entire species of that animal. The terrain that you travel through is typically very natural and very earth-like. Moreover, just to clear up any misconceptions, the shamanic underworld is not associated with anything dark, sinister or evil. That concept belongs to a completely different, often monotheistic religious belief system and cosmology.

A spirit journey to the Lower World is generally undertaken to seek the help and guidance of an animal spirit, to connect with ancestors, to work on the shadow self, to retrieve a power animal for someone else, or for soul retrieval. From a shamanic point of view, anyone who has had a trauma may have had some loss of their soul. From a psychological standpoint, this is called disassociation. One of the classic shamanic methods is to retrieve the lost portion of the soul and return it. When we talk about soul, we are really talking about light. In returning lost soul parts to someone, we are really returning light. To learn more, I recommend reading *Soul Retrieval: Mending the Fragmented Self* by Sandra Ingerman.

The World Tree

The three cosmic realms are linked together by a vertical axis that is commonly referred to as the *axis mundi*, world axis or World Tree. The World Tree could be considered the core fractal of creation which serves to manifest the universe. Images of the World Tree exist in nearly all cultures and represent the world center and/or the connection between heaven and Earth. The *axis mundi* links heaven and Earth as well as providing a path between the two. This central axis of the Cosmos exists within each of us, for we are a fractal of creation.

Through the sound of the drum, which is customarily made of wood from the World Tree, the shaman is transported to the cosmic axis within and conveyed from plane to plane. As Tuvan musicologist Valentina Suzukei explains, "There is a bridge on these sound waves so you can go from one world to another. In the sound world, a tunnel opens through which we can pass, or the shaman's spirits come to us. When you stop playing the drum, the bridge disappears."[4] The inner axis passes through an opening or hole through which the shaman can ascend to the Celestial Realm of unmanifest potential and descend on healing journeys into the temporal realm of manifest form.

Journey technique

To enter a trance state and support your journey, you will need a drum or a shamanic drumming recording.[5] Shamanic drumming is drumming for the purpose of shamanic journeying. A good shamanic drumming recording should be pulsed at around three to four beats per second. You may also rattle, chant or sing to induce trance. There is no right or wrong way to journey. Be innovative and try different ways of journeying. Many people need to move, dance or sing their journeys. My first journeys were supported by listening to a shamanic drumming recording, but now I have stronger journeys when I drum for myself.

Another way to train yourself to focus and concentrate is to narrate your journey as you are experiencing it. To set this up, you need head-phones to listen to the drumming recording and a recorder of some kind. The simultaneous narration and recording technique can be distracting at first, but it is a good way to make sure you are getting all the information your helping spirits are giving you.

For your first journeys, I recommend traveling to the Lower World using the technique taught by the late Michael Harner. Founder of The Foundation for Shamanic Studies, Harner was widely acknowledged as the world's foremost authority on experiential and practical shamanism. In his book, *The Way of the Shaman*, Harner suggests that you visualize an opening into the earth that you remember from sometime in your life. The entrance could be an animal burrow, hollow tree stump, cave, and so on. When the journey begins, you will go down the hole and a tunnel will ap-pear. The tunnel often appears ribbed and may bend or spiral around. This tunnel-like imagery is related to the central axis that links the three inner planes of consciousness. Enter the tunnel and you will emerge into the Lower World, the realm of power animals, spirit guides and ancestral spir-its. It is an earth-like dimension where we can connect with helping spirits.

If you prefer, you can journey to the Upper World, the home of the Thunder Beings and Star Nations. The Celestial Realm is the Loom of Creation and the domain of spirit teachers and divine archetypes such as angels and devas. You can journey to the Upper World to access spiritual guidance and wisdom or to find ways to restore balance in the world. To journey up, you can visualize a tree or ladder that you climb up, soar on the wings of an eagle, or simply lift off the ground and rise into the air. Once you get to the upper realm, the landscape is typically more ethereal, higher in frequency and scintillating in light.

Engaging the imaginal realm

Imagination is our portal to the spirit world. Internal imagery enables us to perceive and connect with the inner realms. If a shaman wants to retrieve information or a lost guardian spirit, "imagining what to look for" is the first step in achieving any result. According to C. Michael Smith, author of *Jung and Shamanism in Dialogue*, "The shaman's journey employs the imagination, and the use of myth as inner map gives the shaman a way of imagining non-ordinary reality, so that he or she may move about intentionally in it."[6] By consciously interacting with the inner imagery, the shaman is able to communicate with spirit guides and power animals. If the shaman is being the hollow bone, the evolution of the journey can be as spontaneous as a dream. The imagery can spill right out the shaman's own life in an imaginal language perhaps only he/she can interpret. And like dreams, journeys can be prescient and revelatory.

Communication in non-ordinary reality is characteristically archetypal, nonverbal and nonlinear in nature. The images we see during a shamanic journey have a universal, primordial quality. Imagery from these experiences is a combination of our imagination and information conveyed to us by the spirits. Our imagination gives the journey a "container" that helps us to understand the messages we receive. It provides us with a way to understand and articulate the experience for ourselves and to others.

The journey process

To perform the following exercise, you will need a drum or a shamanic drumming recording. If you do not have a drum, simply improvise one from available materials; try tapping on an overturned plastic container with a spoon—the larger the container: the deeper the sound. A five-gallon bucket, for example, makes an excellent improvised drum. Read through the exercise first to familiarize yourself with the process. The basic steps for a journey to the Lower World are as follows:

1. Create a purified space, and then open sacred space by calling in the benevolent powers of the seven directions: East, South, West, North, Up, Down and Within. Invoke and ask Spirit Horse to accompany and assist you on your journey. Dim the lights and sit comfortably erect in a chair or on the floor. Close your eyes and ground yourself with some mindful breathing until you are calm and relaxed.
2. Having established sacred space, it is important to form your intention or objective for the journey. It is best to have only one inquiry or question per journey. It is important to focus on the issue that you want to

know more about. Focusing on an issue develops a receptive state of mind and helps you clarify what it is you are truly seeking.

3. After clarifying the intended objective, begin playing a repetitive rhythm that begins slowly, and then gradually builds in intensity to a steady tempo of three to four beats per second (or listen to your shamanic drumming recording). As the drumming begins, close your eyes and focus a moment on the inquiry free of any distractions, emotions or attachments that could distort the response.

4. Next, you should clear your mind of everything. Focused intent, to be effective, should be followed by complete surrender and detachment. Focus your attention on the sound of the drum, thereby stilling the mind. Allow the drum to empty you. Become one with the drum.

5. At this point, you may find it helpful to imagine with all your senses the entrance to a cave, an opening in the earth, or a hollow tree trunk that you have seen or visited. Use an image that you are comfortable with and one that you can clearly visualize. Clear your mind of everything but this image.

6. Approach the entrance or opening and enter it. You may have to pass through some swirling energy, water or fog in order to enter the portal. Typically, you will meet an entity here that will act as your spirit guide. It may appear to you as an animal, a person, a light, a voice, or have no discernable form at all. If you are uncomfortable or put off by whatever appears, ask it to take another form. It is important that you see, feel, hear, or in some way sense the presence of an ally that you trust and feel at ease with before proceeding with your first journey. If you do not, then return through the entrance and journey another time.

7. Pose your query to the guide. Your spirit guide may simply answer your question, but most likely will lead you on a journey. Your guide may become your mount for the journey. Follow your guide's instructions implicitly. If asked to leave, do so at once. Typically, you will proceed down a tunnel at a rapid pace. If you encounter an obstacle, just go over or around it, or look for an opening through it.

8. When you emerge from the passage, you will find yourself in the Lower World. You may be led to a helping spirit that can answer your question. You may go through different landscapes and experience different situations. The possibilities are endless. Just go with the flow and observe whatever happens without trying to analyze anything.

9. When it feels appropriate, gradually slow the tempo of your drumming and retrace your steps back. To achieve this, simply do your journey in reverse. There is no need to rush, and it is not critical that you retrace your route precisely. The reason for retracing your steps is to help you remember the route so that in subsequent journeys you will be able to travel to and from the Lower World with greater ease and efficiency. Upon your return to the entrance, thank your guide, emerge from the opening and return to your body.

10. Once you have returned to ordinary reality, end your drum journey with four strong beats to signal that the sacred time of focus is ended. If you are listening to a shamanic drumming recording, most recordings have a similar call back signal near the end of the track, followed by a short period of rapid drumming to assist you in refocusing your awareness back to your physical body. If for any reason you want to come back before the call back, just retrace your steps back. Sit quietly for a few moments, and then open your eyes.

It would be advisable to record your journey in a journal as soon as you have returned to ordinary reality. Journeys, like dreams, tend to fade quickly from conscious awareness. Very little may happen on your first journeys. You may only experience darkness. When this happens, simply try again at a different time. Shamanic journey work is a learned skill that improves with practice. The key is to practice and to establish a long-term relationship with your spirit guides.

Ecstatic trance postures

I highly recommend incorporating ecstatic trance postures into your journey work. Some of my most profound trance experiences have taken place while holding shamanic body postures. Anthropologist Felicitas Goodman discovered that specific yoga-like poses recur in the art and artifacts of world cultures, even societies widely separated by time and space. Goodman's hypothesis, therefore, was that these postures represented coded instructions on how to produce consistent trance-like effects. Goodman researched and explored ritual body postures as a means to achieve a bodily induced trance experience. Her studies led her to many countries and to trying out these body positions practically with hundreds of participants worldwide. She discovered that people who assume these body postures report strikingly similar trance experiences regardless of their worldview or belief systems.

These postures produce a common effect, according to Goodman, because they all share one thing in common: the human body, the basic structure and functioning of which has remained unchanged since the time of our most ancient ancestors. The nervous and endocrine systems are, in fact, all much the same as they were 30,000 years ago, a fact which enables contemporary urban dwellers to enter non-ordinary reality as effectively, and through the same neural doorways, as shamans throughout history. Combined with shamanic drumming, the postures engender a profound change in consciousness, leading to new insights into healing, inner development and soul purpose. There are different postures that facilitate healing, divination, shapeshifting, spirit journeys, and more.

Goodman identified several prerequisites for a successful trance posture experience, many of which will be familiar to you from your standard shamanic journey:

1. Preparing oneself spiritually, mentally and physically;
2. Establishing a sacred space with intention and respect;
3. Quieting the mind through meditation and breathing practices;
4. Inducing a trance state with a repetitive rhythm on a drum or rattle;
5. Holding a specific trance posture for at least fifteen minutes.

The South American Lower World posture

To introduce you to trance postures, I have selected a spirit journeying posture from Belinda Gore's book, *Ecstatic Body Postures: An Alternate Reality Book*. This posture originated among the Jivaro people of Ecuador for taking the shamanic journey to the Lower World. Using this posture is the easiest way to make the journey to the lower realms. According to Gore, one of Dr. Goodman's prominent students, "Most people find their way to the Lower World using this posture whether they visualize the entrance at the outset or not."[7] People often report feeling a cool, invigorating sensation as they make their descent. It is not unusual for people to experience various kinds of healing while holding this posture. It is also common for people to see a lot of spirit animals.

In preparation for the trance, take a few minutes to practice the posture so that your body feels comfortable in that position. Turn off the cell phone and make whatever arrangements are necessary to assure that you will not be disturbed during the trance. Prepare a purified sacred space and ground yourself with some mindful breathing. To induce a trance, you will need a shamanic drumming recording ready to go at a volume that is appropriate. When you are ready, turn on the recording and assume the posture.

To assume this posture, lie down on your back on the floor (or on a mat) with your legs fully extended. You can place a small pillow under your knees to alleviate any back discomfort. Do not, however, place anything under your head that would elevate it. Stretch your right arm out along your side in a natural, relaxed position. Raise your left arm and rest the back of your left open hand on the middle of your forehead. Make sure that you are not putting any pressure on your eyes, and your eyes should be closed.

During the trance, your only task is to remain in the correct position and to stay aware of what you are experiencing. Focus your attention on the sound of the drum and allow the drum to empty you. Become one with the drum. If your mind wanders, bring the focus of your attention back to the beat of the drum. Following the sound of the drum restores your focus and leads your body back into a trance state. When you hear the call back signal on the recording, move out of the posture and sit quietly for a few moments. After the trance, get plenty of rest and drink a lot of water. Avoid any kind of focused or intense activity for the rest of the day, and get a good night's sleep.

What you will experience

Ecstatic trance is not always what many people anticipate it to be, and sometimes there may be doubt that anything at all takes place. There are, however, some key indicators that confirm a transcendent state of consciousness. Once you enter a trance state, the rhythm or sound of the drum tends to change. The drumbeat may appear to speed up or slow down while the sound may grow louder, softer or disappear. You may experience a change in body temperature, feel energy flowing through your body, or find yourself twitching, swaying or rocking. It is not uncommon to hear sounds or voices. You may even smell specific aromas. You may see colorful patterns, symbolic images or dreamlike visions. Some people may find that they have a highly developed inner vision, whereas others may rely more on an inner voice of insight or an inner feeling of certainty. Be prepared to experience ecstatic trance with any of your senses. The key is to observe whatever happens without trying to analyze the experience.

Understanding trance journeys

Shamanic journeying is not an exceptional skill reserved for certain people, but knowing what to do with intuition, how to respond to it, and how to integrate it into day-to-day life is an exceptional skill that can, and should, be learned. It is important to release any expectations you may have about what a journey should be like. Too often people reject what they are legitimately experiencing because it does not fit their expectations of what should be happening. The key is to trust that what is happening is exactly what is meant to occur at that moment in time.

Like the shaman, you will find the spirit world to be a fountain of wisdom and power. It is understood that what takes place in the journey world will follow in ordinary reality. Insights gained there shift thinking and behavior here. Healing which transpires there creates healing here. The most empowering gift shamanic journeying offers each of us is direct revelation that manifests as visions, inner voices or experiences with our own spirit helpers.

Once you achieve a state of ecstatic communion, how do you know you are listening to your spirit guides and not just making it up? Here are some suggestions on distinguishing spirit guides from your own inner voice:

1. The form or tone of the message sounds different than your inner voice;
2. The information is something you could not have known or expected;
3. The information is something you may not want to hear;
4. The message brings a smile to your face or tears to your eyes;
5. The message creates an "a-ha" moment of realization.

Ultimately it does not matter whether the information comes from your helping spirits, your imagination or your higher self. What matters is the value and practicality of the guidance and if it benefits you and the community. For me, shamanic journey work begins with my willingness to trust the guidance from within.

To better understand your journeys, I recommend recording your experiences in a journal as soon as you have returned to ordinary reality.

Trance experiences, like dreams, tend to fade quickly from conscious awareness. Journaling is a contemplative practice that can help you become more aware of your inner life and feel more connected to your experiences and the world around you. Keeping a journal provides a record of your spiritual growth and allows you to reflect upon and better interpret journeys. In some cases, your journey experiences will be clear and easy to understand. At other times, your journey may be dreamlike and full of symbolism. Interpret such journeys as you would any dream. Look for possible associations related to each symbol or image. Do not overanalyze the journey, for its meaning will become clear at the appropriate time.

Not every journey you undertake will necessarily be coherent, vivid or powerful. Still, no matter how esoteric or random the experience may seem, it augments your shamanic skill and knowledge. Seemingly insignificant events in a journey or vision may manifest in a powerful way in your ordinary state of awareness. Be on the lookout for synchronicities, for they confirm that your shamanic work is producing effects beyond the bounds of probability or coincidence.

The more you practice shamanic journeying, the better you will get at it. Nothing may happen on your first journeys. You may not be able to turn off the mind chatter or go anywhere. When this happens, simply try again at a different time. Eventually you will be able to take a rapid inner journey anywhere or anytime the need arises. The regular practice of journeying into the spirit world changes you. It broadens your viewpoint, helps you to let go of judgment, encourages you to value yourself more and makes living your life more manageable. It gives you equilibrium.

Dangers of shamanic journeying

Shamanic journeying is not without its risks. It is not a practice to be taken lightly, and one should not attempt it unless they have a comprehensive understanding of grounding techniques. Otherwise, it can sometimes be quite difficult to fully ground yourself into your body and restore self-awareness. It is possible to journey too much and spend too much time out of your body in other realms. It can leave one feeling ungrounded and disconnected from life on the physical plane. It is important to have an energetic balance between the spiritual and physical. The dangers of shamanic practice arise when one attempts a certain level of shamanic technique when not sufficiently ready for it. The function of consistent, regular practice is to develop the skills and talents so that shamanic practitioners do not unintentionally hurt themselves or others. Shamanic practice requires discipline, concentration and purpose.

Shamanic journeying involves dissolving the boundaries of how we normally interact with the world. The comfort we derive from the familiarity of ordinary reality gives way when we enter non-ordinary reality. If doing this brings up intense emotions that feel uncomfortable, threatening or out of control, then I suggest stopping. If you have a known history of dissociation or psychosis, then there is the potential for those symptoms to be triggered by such an experience. In that case, it would be best to consult a shamanic practitioner who is trained in such matters. When we are not fully in our bodies, we are disconnected from personal boundaries, sense of self and the wisdom held within our bodies. It makes us more vulnerable to any non-benevolent beings that exist in other realms.

So how can we protect ourselves when we take a shamanic journey? Always begin by creating a purified sacred space where you are protected and safe. I also recommend that you wear prayer ties and spritz yourself with holy water for blessing and protection. Open sacred space by invoking the benevolent powers of the seven directions, and then call out to your helping spirits for help and protection. It is very important to take a trusted spirit guide with you when journeying. Your spirit guide knows the spirit world well and will lead, assist and protect you when necessary. When taking a shamanic journey, you will meet an entity at the entrance to the spirit world that will act as your guide. Once you meet your own power animal, you can call upon it to accompany you on your journeys.

Beyond that, for a studied shamanic practitioner, the dangers are relatively few as long as you adhere to a few simple rules: always ask permission before doing any healing work, offer gratitude to any and all beings that assist you in your work, be clear with your intentions and objectives, be respectful of the Earth and all our relations, and do not dabble. If you are not ready for deep spiritual work, hard truths and serious accountability, then this may not be the right path for you.

The ethics of shamanic healing

In shamanic work, there is one essential ethical requirement—permission. According to Susan Mokelke, who leads the Foundation for

Shamanic Studies, "Permission means the express, informed consent of the client for a specific individual or group to perform shamanic healing or divination—including the consent to disclose any information about the client."[8] Healing without permission is not only unethical, but deviates into the realm of sorcery and black magic. It is unethical because it is every person's right and responsibility to decide what to do in matters relating to his or her own soul.

If the healee is in a coma, permission should be obtained from the person's closest living relative or guardian before doing shamanic work of any sort. Even then, you should still journey to ask that person's soul what healing, if any, they wish to have done.

Before doing psychopomp work, or other mediation involving the soul of a deceased person, you still need to get permission from his or her next of kin. When you journey to help a deceased person, you should ask their soul what assistance, if any they want. When in doubt, do not perform the work.

Even in cases of natural disasters and crises, it is essential to get permission from the spirits of the land or people involved before trying to help. When doing long distance or remote healing, it is important to do only the work that was requested and to work closely with your helping spirits.

10 good reasons to take a shamanic journey

1. To meet your power animal: Now that you are familiar with the basics of shamanic journeying, you can travel to the Lower World with the intention of meeting and acquiring your power animal or guardian spirit. The key to recognizing your power animal is that it will repeatedly appear to you at least four times. It may appear to you at different angles, in different aspects, or as different animals of the same species. After an animal has presented itself to you four times, ask the spirit animal to be your ally, to merge with your being. Imagine yourself embracing the animal, and then return rapidly to ordinary reality. Envision bringing the animal spirit back with you. Your power animal will readily return with you, or else it would not have revealed itself.

2. To connect with your inner or spirit self: Shamanic journeying heightens the ability of perception and enables you to see into the deeper realms of the self. The moment you bond with your spirit is the

moment your heart opens. The first time you glimpse your spirit self, you gasp and cry. You know who you are. That is the moment you begin to heal. Journey work connects you to your core, enhancing your sense of empowerment, and stimulating your creative expression.

3. To experience healing: From a shamanic perspective illness manifests on an emotional or physical level due to spiritual imbalance or disharmony. We can journey within to work directly with the emotional and spiritual aspects of the self so that healing can occur. A journey can shed light on a health issue and provide clues as to what is needed for full healing to take place. Journey work is also an effective way to stimulate the release of suppressed feelings and emotional trauma in order to heal. The process restores emotional health through expression and integration of emotions.

4. To clarify life purpose: When we are unaware of our soul's true purpose, or simply not aligned in our actions, we often experience a malaise of the spirit. We can engage the blueprint of our soul path through the vehicle of journeying. Shamanic journeying is a time-tested medium for individual self-realization. We can journey within to access wisdom and energies that can help awaken our soul calling and restore us to wholeness. Journey practice connects us with our deepest core values and our highest vision of who we are and why we are here. It heightens our sense of mission and purpose, empowering our personal evolution.

5. To divine information: You can journey within to obtain information about personal and community issues. Your helping spirits are a good resource when it comes to answering questions pertaining to relationships, health issues, or any issue. To divine information in a journey, begin with a clear question that you would like to ask of your helping spirits. Decide which of your helping spirits you would like to answer your question, and then journey to the place where you normally meet them in non-ordinary reality. Of course you can ask your question to as many of your helping spirits as you wish. When divining on behalf of others, it is vital that you have their permission.

6. To connect with benevolent ancestors: The desire to communicate with our ancestors is an innate part of the human experience. Benevolent ancestral spirits can guide, protect and heal the living. Your ancestors and the collective spiritual power of all those who went before you reside in the Lower World. If you embark on a journey

with the intention of connecting with those who have passed, they may come to meet you. Keep in mind that spirits choose to come into relationship with the person seeking. You can seek ancestral spirits, but the spirits must choose.

7. To prepare for death: Shamans believe that learning to leave the physical body is important, for without this experience, the soul may become confused after death and remain stuck in the Middle World. When a person dies, there is usually a smooth transition into the afterlife, but when a person suffers a traumatic death, they may not have an awareness of who and where they are. This makes it difficult for them to make their journey to the afterlife. Other souls linger in the space between life and the afterlife for fear of going to hell. Sadly, most of the psychopomp rites of passage that once helped prepare a person for death have disappeared. Hence, journeying is one of the most important shamanic skills that we can develop. By journeying to the Lower World, the place to which human souls travel upon physical death, we can prepare for our own death.

8. To connect with the Thunder Beings: Because of the turmoil in the world today, it would be beneficial if more of us established an intimate relationship with the Thunder Beings who exist in the Upper World. Through lightning, they directly purify the air we breathe, the water we drink, and the Earth we cultivate. The Thunder Beings are the force behind all weather changes and sustain life on Earth. Their medicine and gift is balance, change and renewal. Thunder Beings create a storm to overcome static tensions, clearing the way for the rainbow of peace and harmony. The greater the obstructions to harmony, the more destructive the storm must be to clear away those obstructions. The Thunder Beings are a force for both dissolution and creation. According to Taoist adept and Thunder-specialist Samudranath, through the Thunder Beings, "all life has been initiated or created, is sustained, and will be destroyed. In all traditions it is Thunder-beings who govern nature and all life; they are the Creators. They sustain balanced life, and destroy imbalance, the cause of suffering."[9]

9. To work on the shadow self: We can journey to the Lower World to explore the shadow realm of the subconscious—those unwanted aspects of the self that we have denied and suppressed. The shadow self consists mostly of negative human emotions and impulses like desire, greed, envy, jealousy and rage. Whatever inferior qualities we deny in

ourselves become part of the disowned self. When we do not pay attention to the dark side of our personality, it has a way of influencing our behavior. We say and do things that we later regret. Through journeying, we can engage in an inner dialogue with our shadow side and integrate it into our conscious selves. As we integrate our shadow side, we become more whole and mature. Shadow work can lead to greater authenticity and creativity, clearer perception, enhanced energy, psychological integration and personal awakening. That said, perhaps the most compelling reason to journey is...

10. To find ways to restore balance in the world: The Upper or Celestial Realm is the archetypal cosmological matrix of the universe. This divine blueprint forms the matrix of possibilities that correspond to the world we experience through our mind and senses. When harmony between the human realm and the original intended blueprint is disturbed, we can journey to the Upper World to bring back the balance. We can also go there to acquire archetypal knowledge, to bring a vision into being, or to influence events in the material world. By interacting with the archetypes, we interact with their counterparts in the outer material world.

Chapter 7

Becoming the Hollow Bone

When we become hollow bones there is no limit to what the higher powers can do in and through us in spiritual things.
—Frank Fools Crow, Oglala Lakota holy man[1]

To restore our broken reality, we can become the hollow bone. The shaman has sometimes been described as being a hollow bone, one who can enter an altered state of consciousness without their personal ego. This non-ego hollowness makes a way for spirit to use them as a healing instrument. In this way, the shaman is a channel for higher consciousness.

The hollow bone teaching is an ancient meditative practice, found under different names in Buddhism, Taoism, shamanism and Native American spirituality. It is a way to shift your consciousness to become an empty vessel for spirit. The idea is to become a conduit for the light. When we can move our ego and rational mind out of the way to channel the divine power of the universe through us, all healing is possible.

This teaching is embodied in the eagle bone whistle, which is carved from the hollow wing bone of an eagle.[2] The whistle is used in certain Native American ceremonies for invoking the spirit of the eagle and for opening a path of communication between the spiritual and earthly realms. It is a sacred instrument connecting the two worlds, the non-physical with the physical.

The way of the hollow bone

The venerated, late Oglala Lakota holy man Frank Fools Crow taught that you must become like a hollow bone to be a great healer. According to Fools Crow, "We are called to become hollow bones for our people, and anyone else we can help, and we are not supposed to seek power for our personal use and honor. What we bones really become is the pipeline that connects Wakan Tanka [whom we could call the Creator, Great Mystery, or Tao], the Helpers and the community together."[3]

In his becoming a hollow bone, Fools Crow believed that he went through four stages: First, he called in Great Mystery to rid himself of anything that would impede him in any way, such as doubt, questions or reluctance. Then he recognized himself as a clean tube, ready to be filled with hope, possibilities, and anxious to be filled with power. He experienced the power as it came surging into him. Finally, giving the power away to others, and knowing that as he is emptied out, the higher powers will keep filling him with even greater power to be given away.

It takes years of dedicated and disciplined practice to become a true hollow bone. It is an ongoing process—a ceaseless journey. You must take time every day to observe what is blocking the flow of your life force energy. Ask yourself questions like: How am I stuck? What is blocking me? What am I resisting? What am I afraid of? When you observe something that is blocking you, do not try to analyze or resolve it. Simply observe whatever comes up without judgment or attachment.

This is analogous to the Taoist practice of non-doing. Non-doing is not a withdrawal from action, but rather a non-attachment to the actions and intentions you choose during your life. You must release all attachments to anything that would block the flow of your vital energy in any way, such as expectations, preconceptions or rigid beliefs. Rigid thinking will only keep you stuck in a narrow perspective, distorting your perceptions of reality. Rigidity is resistance, and resistance will shut you down, block your connection with inner truth, and prevent you from seeing the true nature of the universe. There is wisdom in letting go and going with the flow.

Reaping the benefits

Meditative practices of all kinds are an important part of the ongoing task of keeping our insides clean, but hollow bone meditation, combined with drumming, also facilitates a transcendent state of unity consciousness. True enlightenment means feeling and recognizing our true oneness with everything else—reaching a state of unity consciousness. According to a recent study, sixty percent of Americans believe they have had a mystical experience in which they felt a sense of unity with all things.

The benefits of this state of unity consciousness include a deep sense of relaxation, healing, more personal energy, better memory, greater mental clarity and enhanced creativity. Feelings of peacefulness, timelessness and spiritual well-being are common, along with a oneness of feeling and purpose with the totality of a vast, singular, interrelated universe. When we feel that deep oneness we are ecstatic. Ecstasy does not necessarily mean joy or bliss; it is the feeling of oneness. Becoming a hollow bone is a simple and effective way to induce this profound state of consciousness.

Becoming a hollow bone

To become a hollow bone, try the following exercise. To perform the exercise, you will need a drum or a shamanic drumming recording. Read through the exercise first to familiarize yourself with the process.

1. Create a purified space, and then ritually open sacred space by calling in the benevolent powers of the seven directions: East, South, West, North, Up, Down and Within. Dim the lights and sit comfortably erect in a chair or on the floor. Close your eyes and ground yourself with some mindful breathing.
2. When you are fully relaxed, ask your helping spirits and the higher powers to remove any blockages that prevent you from functioning as a hollow bone. Repeat the affirmation, "I choose to be a clean, hollow bone." Visualize yourself as a hollow bone or tube that is all shiny on the inside and empty. The cleaner the bone, the more energy you can channel through it, and the faster it will flow.
3. The next step is to enter a trance state. Begin drumming a slow, steady heartbeat rhythm, and then gradually build in intensity to a tempo of three to four beats per second (or listen to your shamanic drumming recording). The steady lub-dub, lub-dub of a heartbeat rhythm generates yin energy, which is magnetic and receptive in nature. Yin energy is a descending force that draws the energy of the original cosmological pattern down into the earthly realm, helping to align the circle of life with the original intention for the Earth. One of the commonly held beliefs in shamanic cultures is that there exists a patterned cosmological order, which can be disrupted by human activity.
4. As you drum, imagine the unifying spirit of the divine source flowing through you. Visualize a beam of white light flowing down from above, entering your hollow bone, and traveling down into the earth. You may feel it, see it, sense it, or simply imagine it. As you focus on it, it will occur, for energy and life force follow thought. Allow spirit to flow into and embody you so that the speed and rhythm of your

playing come under its control. As Tuvan shaman Sailyk-ool Kanchyyp-ool describes it, "I am not myself. But, I am being maneuvered by the spirits. They tell me. 'Beat hard, beat fast, beat a long beat.' And they also tell me when to stop."[4]

5. As the drum meditation evolves, you will become more ecstatic, and spirit will perhaps create new rhythms. You are now moving into a higher state of universal consciousness and developing a new shamanic skill. At higher levels, a healer becomes adept at detaching all sense of self, fully present in the moment, as a hollow bone or living conduit for healing energy to move through.

6. When it feels appropriate (or when you hear the call back signal on the shamanic drumming recording), gradually slow the tempo of your drumming to draw your consciousness back into your body. Do not rush the transformation. Visualize yourself fully grounded in your body, and then slowly open your eyes. Once you have returned to ordinary reality, end your drum meditation with four strong beats to signal that the sacred time of focus is ended. Sit quietly for a few moments, and then open your eyes.

The magic of the hollow bone

As you will find, the effects of becoming a conduit for the source of existence are seldom subtle. Expect sometimes dramatic physical responses and emotional releases. We tend to impede the flow of this vital energy, thereby depleting our personal power. Self-limiting belief, fear, doubt and resistance constrict the energy channels in the body. By "hollowing out" or emptying ourselves of limiting beliefs, we remove all obstructions to the flow of source energy. The magic of the hollow bone lies in allowing the divine source to work through us, rather than resisting it with our learned limitations. In becoming a clear channel for divine energy and wisdom, all healing is possible.

10 good reasons to become a hollow bone

1. To restore and sustain the order of existence: The Upper or Celestial Realm is the archetypal matrix of the universe. This patterned cosmological order has been greatly disturbed by human activity. By becoming a hollow bone, we can channel the energy of the original intended

pattern down into the physical realm, restoring the archetypal cosmological state.

2. To bring our lives into harmony with the ultimate reality of the universe: Taoists believe that by dwelling in harmony with the Cosmos,
one may attain a state of such inner clarity and insight that all actions
become synchronous and spontaneously correct. Such a person knows
what to do by abiding in a state of quietism, by letting go of all
worldly thought so that the creative force of the Cosmos may enter
their minds and bodies. Such accord with the Tao allows one to accomplish things without effort. One attains a state of optimal or flow
experience. It is a way that channels creative energy into one's work
and everyday life.

3. To live a longer and happier life: By emptying ourselves of self-
concern and entering into stillness, the higher powers can flow through
us unobstructed. It is an effective way to restore our mind-body-spirit
to a natural state of bliss that connects us to our essential nature and
who we really are. This method was so powerful that the famous Taoist medicine doctor Sun Simiao, who himself lived to be over a hundred years old, wrote: "Tranquility then attains to concentration, and
the body continues to exist for years eternal."[5]

4. To attain a state of emptiness: Taoists believe that we must empty ourselves to achieve ultimate self-realization. To reach such a state, however, is a life-long process. One should live an active life and experience many things in order to satisfy one's curiosities, yearnings and
desires. Try everything in moderation. By satisfying your involvement
with them, you rid your life of distractions, opening wider the access
to the Tao, or mysterious void. This inner need for expression must be
fulfilled in order to reach emptiness. When we attain a state of emptiness, we create a void. This allows the eternal Tao to fill the void, for
Tao can only gather in the void.

5. To surrender the ego: Surrendering the ego means to identify with the
soul, not with the body and personality. The subjugation of the ego is a
necessary step towards enlightenment. When we become a hollow
bone, we relinquish the ego's control of our mind, thoughts and actions. We give up the need for control. When we surrender the ego's
agendas, we merge with divine will and become an instrument of the
light. Ultimately the role of every person in this world is to become a
conduit for the light.

6. To enter into inner silence: In silence we can hear our own inner voice and discover the truth within. When there is inner silence, there is time for deep introspection and to allow the true self to speak. Silence is the source of everything; the gateway to inner knowing. Silence creates the resonance of contemplation, insight and direct communication with the source.

7. To see through illusions: When we become a hollow bone, we begin to see through the illusions that have held us captive within ego consciousness. We finally see through the illusions of duality, separation and scarcity, which produce all human suffering. When these limiting beliefs are relinquished, we can recognize our true oneness with everything else. We discover that there is only energy; infinite and eternal.

8. To become an instrument of creation: When we drum, we open portals to the spirit world, draw spirit in, and open ourselves up to receive it. In opening ourselves up, we become a conduit of divine knowing energy. Our actions then spring from divine will rather than the ego. We become a direct participant in the evolution of creation. We are the Creator, here in living flesh, for this world.

9. To become a spiritual intercessor: A spiritual intercessor is someone who mediates between the physical and spiritual worlds, acting as a messenger, healer and advisor to the community. By becoming the hollow bone, we become the conduit that connects the Cosmos to the community. We harmonize the cosmic and the terrestrial. We become the bridge that unites the earthly (body), human (mind), and heavenly (spirit) realms. We integrate inner and outer experiences, bringing the body, mind and spirit into harmonious accord.

10. To experience perfect communion with all of life: By becoming a hollow bone, we move from feeling separate to a profound sense of connectedness; from the personal to the global. This experience of mystical union with the Cosmos is said, by many of the world's spiritual traditions, to be the final realization. Consciousness rediscovers its true nature and recognizes itself in all things. Taoists believe that when the human mind resonates with the mind of Tao, it will be enlightened and even nourish the mind of Tao, and the harmony between the two minds will benefit all of creation.

Chapter 8

Changing the World

The more aware of your intentions and your experiences you become, the more you will be able to connect the two, and the more you will be able to create the experiences of your life consciously. This is the development of mastery. It is the creation of authentic power.
—Gary Zukav, American spiritual teacher and author[1]

Whether you realize it or not, you are creating your reality all the time. Your reality is the perfect, exact mirror of your thoughts and what you consistently focus upon. Every thought, idea, or image in the mind has form and substance. Everything that we perceive began with a thought. The structure of our universe is thought, mind and consciousness. Consciousness determines the form of our experience. Consciousness is the "theater of perceptual awareness." It is the collective consciousness of humanity that shapes physical reality. We are the universe made conscious to experience itself. We are mind. We live in a universe of mind. From photons to galaxies, life is conscious intelligent energy that can form itself into any pattern or function.

Metaphysically, the ultimate nature of existence is that there is but one consciousness which presides over a singular, yet multidimensional, field of energy that it can form into any patterns it desires by the exercise of its thoughts and intentions. And these patterns encompass everything seen and unseen. This consciousness has been referred to as source consciousness, universal consciousness, or cosmic consciousness. Moreover, cosmic consciousness not only creates patterns of energy, it can also perceive and experience them.

There is only consciousness, information and the perception of information, and this facilitates the creation and experience of multiple realities. The world that you believe exists outside of you is basically an illusion—it is a purely perceptual experience. Your experiences are real, but the outer world is imaginary. Your reality is only information that was imagined into existence and is essentially just imagery that your consciousness perceives. Perception is an illusory product of consciousness.

The world around you is nothing more than a very convincing perceptual illusion.

Awaken into the dream

In her essay "Awakening into Dreamtime: The Shaman's Journey," Wynne Hanner explores the Australian Aboriginal concept of Dreamtime as a source of and guide to transforming our own world view. According to Aboriginal mythology, Dreamtime is a sacred era in which ancestral spirit beings formed The Creation. Indigenous Australians believe the world is real only because it has been dreamed into being. As Hanner explains in her essay, "The Aborigines embrace the concept of 'reality dreaming,' with reality and Dreamtime intertwined. Reality can be illusion, deception, learning, perception, experience, and is the evolution of consciousness in the alchemy of time. Reality shifts and changes like the flow of the collective unconscious, and is in constant motion creating new spiral patterns of experience. Reality, in its illusion, is the dream from which we all awaken. To understand and work with these concepts is to awaken into the dream."[2]

The Aborigines are reminding us that what we are experiencing is a dream—a cosmic play. We are being invited to awaken into the dream and recognize that the condition of our soul is reflected in the collective dream of everyday life. When the soul is in a state of discontent, conflict and discord, these conditions manifest in our daily life's events as dissonance, confusion, ill health and misfortune. Conversely, when our soul is in a state of peace and harmony, these qualities manifest in our life as ease and acceptance, caring and accord with the world around us. From an Aboriginal perspective, the restoration of one's soul contributes to the restoration of the collective soul of humanity.

Creating reality

We are creating our reality with our thoughts, beliefs, intentions, and more. When we are oblivious to the power that we all share to create our collective reality, that power slips away from us and our reality becomes a nightmare. We begin to feel like victims of a dark and chaotic creation that we are unable to influence or change. We are inundated with negative world events that create anxiety, fear and hopelessness. The only way to end this dreadful reality is to awaken to the fact that it is imaginary, and recognize our ability to imagine a better story, one that the universe will work with us to manifest.

We cannot "restore" our broken reality without "restorying" our life. It is easy to create in the world that everyone believes to be true, the collective story of humanity. It is easy to reproduce and replicate the reality of the world as we know it; in fact, it is automatic. It requires no thought or awareness. We can only change our collective story by changing the way we think—by changing our beliefs, expectations and assumptions which keep us stuck in a limited perspective of our personal and social reality. Those aspects of our experience that are most enduring are the effect of habitual expectations and beliefs, or in other words, what we focus our attention on.

It is through our attention that we influence and direct the aspects of our experience and the world around us. What we pay attention to becomes what we know as ourselves and our world, for energy flows where attention goes. As positive psychologist Mihaly Csikszentmihalyi points out in his book, *Flow: The Psychology of Optimal Experience*, "We create ourselves by how we invest this energy. Memories, thoughts, and feelings are all shaped by how we use it. And it is an energy under our control; hence, attention is our most important tool in the task of improving the quality of experience."[3] What we focus our attention on is what our life becomes—the clearer the intention, the greater the impact.

Drumming with intention

Our creative potential is far greater than we realize—we all possess the power to manifest our intentions. Shamanic drumming is a time-tested technique for transforming our intentions into reality. The drum serves as a concentration device for stilling the mind and focusing our attention. Shamans have understood for centuries that sustained focused attention on a specific intention, while in a state of inner silence, allows your intent to penetrate the celestial matrix of being that generates and nurtures all forms. Such attention channels the creative energy of the universe into manifesting the physical equivalent of the focus.

You can focus your intention on anything. Your conscious intent may be to heal yourself, someone else, or the planet. You may wish to manifest divine qualities such as compassion, empathy, and altruism or bring more light into the world. You could ask for the power to manifest your full potential, talents and purpose, or simply ask for whatever guidance or knowledge you need at this time. Be mindful, however, of the motives underlying your intent. Intentions motivated by malice, greed, envy, and the like are seldom fruitful and will only block your spiritual growth.

To clarify what it is you truly need, it is helpful to word your intention in a concise and clear-cut manner. You must be specific about what you want to accomplish. Articulating your desired outcome is how you channel the energy of the drumming toward the intended objective. Reciting a descriptive word or phrase will help sustain your focus as well as provide a clear pattern which the power of the universe can express into manifestation. It is important to affirm your intention with belief and expectation. You must eliminate all doubt and trust the creative power of your intent. The keynote of intent is that all you will ever need exists as potential and is waiting to manifest. The following exercise is designed to acquaint you with this process.

Four-round drumming

When drumming with intention, I like to use a four-round drumming, consisting of a prayer, healing, thank you and closing round. I use four rounds because four is a sacred number in indigenous shamanic practices. All events and actions are based on this number, because everything was created in fours. The Great Mystery reveals itself as the powers of the four directions and these four powers provide the organizing principle for everything that exists in the world. There are four winds, four seasons, four elements, four phases of the moon, four stages to humanity's spiritual evolution, and so on.

For instance, the Native American sweat lodge ceremony (Inipi) is usually carried out in four rounds. The whole process is modeled after the Medicine Wheel, which is a universal symbol that can be found in many indigenous cultures around the world. The Medicine Wheel, sometimes known as the Sacred Hoop, represents the natural cycles of life and the basic way in which the natural world moves and evolves. The Medicine Wheel represents the archetypal journey each of us takes in life. This journey has four stages or rounds, each associated with a cardinal direction. Four rounds signify completion, wholeness or fullness.

To perform this exercise, you will need a drum. Read through the exercise first to familiarize yourself with the process. The steps are as follows:

1. Create a purified space, and then open sacred space by calling in the spiritual energies of the seven directions: East, South, West, North, Up, Down and Within. Invoke and ask your helping spirits to be with you and to help you connect with them. Dim the lights and sit comfortably erect in a chair or on the floor. Close your eyes and ground yourself with some mindful breathing until you are calm and relaxed.

2. Form your intention, or intended objective, and then begin the "prayer" round of drumming. A steady eagle-beat pulsed at three to four beats per second is the most effective. The eagle-beat is projective in nature and will carry your intention and prayers to the archetypal Celestial Realm, causing the "Tapestry of Creation" to reweave itself in accordance with those prayers.

3. Now focus on your intention to seed the blueprint of the desired outcome. As you focus on it, it will occur, for energy and life force follow thought. It is best to stroke the drum firmly, yet gently, producing ringing tones and overtones. Move the drumstick around the drumhead as you play. If you can, find the drum's sweet spot, that place where the drum begins to talk, hum and sing. Work the drum to build up the humming overtones. These are the best frequencies for healing and raising your vibration. The whole drum needs to sing.

4. As you drum, repeat the words of your intention over and over like a mantra. Reciting a mantra into the drum charges it with energy and informs the drum's spirit of your intention. Sustain your focus until you sense that your intention has penetrated the archetypal matrix that forms and shapes our reality. There are several key indicators that confirm you have connected to the Celestial Realm and seeded the blueprint of the desired outcome. The sound of the drum tends to change. The drum's pitch, timbre, or volume may appear to rise or fall. Another indication is a change in resonance. The sound of the overtones tends to intensify to a crescendo, gradually increasing in volume until a climactic connection is made, and then subsiding. With time and practice, you will learn to sense and interpret such subtle indicators.

5. Once your intention has been seeded, begin the "healing" round of drumming. Stroke a slow, steady heartbeat rhythm, gradually increasing the tempo and intensity. This healing pulse is magnetic and

receptive in nature, drawing awareness, archetypal knowledge and transpersonal powers down into the material world. It gives form and substance to the seed of your intention.

6. As you drum, clear your mind of everything. Paradoxically, focused intent must be followed by complete surrender and detachment to be effective. You must relinquish completely both the specifics of your goal and how that goal is to be achieved. The unknowable powers of the universe will create what is needed, often in a most unpredictable way. You must be confident that the outcome, while out of your own hands, is in the process of being changed or created.

7. If your intention is for healing, for yourself or someone else, then merely let the drum do the healing. Become like a hollow bone, and allow the spirit of your drum to embody you so that your playing comes under its control. When embodying spirits, they will actually dictate the rhythm and speed until you reach something that is suitable for them. The drum's spirit will channel and direct healing energy based solely on your original intention.

8. Sustain the heartbeat rhythm for as long as you feel it is appropriate. It is best to trust your intuition in this process. Each person must ultimately go within to find their own internal timing.

9. When you feel the power ebbing, begin the "thank you" round of drumming. Drum once again the even cadence of the eagle-beat. Sustain a steady tempo of three to four beats per second while giving thanks to all your relations for the needs met. The rhythm of the drum will carry your gratitude into the archetypal realm.

10. Finally, end your drumming with four strong beats to signal that the sacred time of focus is ended. When you have finished your spiritual work, sacred space should be closed.

I have found this drum method to be very effective in a myriad of situations. Feel free, however, to adapt it to serve your own needs. Rhythm is a very personal thing. Experiment with different tempos and improvise new rhythms. Rhythm is the carrier of the specific intention of the ritual.

Changing the world

If consciousness creates reality, then change starts within. It starts with the way you observe the outer world from your inner world. You can change the outer world by changing your inner world. The world is your stage. The stage that collective reality plays out on is just there to create a context within which to play out the story of your personal reality. You can create anything you want in life, and it is not limited to what already exists in the collective reality, but it does provide a host of options to select into your life. However, they are all optional—they cannot enter into your experience unless you invite them in with your thoughts. In fact, the collective reality can be a distraction that lures you into focusing on "what is" instead of "what can be."

Quantum physics points out that this is a participatory universe in which the power to change reality is literally in our hands at every moment. Modern physics is describing what indigenous shamans have long known. Shamans know that the creative matrix of the universe exists within human consciousness, enabling humans to participate in creation itself. For the shaman, changing reality is not just an ability, but also a duty one must perform so that future generations will inherit a world where they can live in peace, harmony and abundance.

Shamans access the creative matrix through techniques of ecstasy such as drumming. Rhythmic drumming is a simple and effective way to induce an ecstatic trance state. Shamanic drumming transports you to the creative matrix within. It is an inward spiritual journey of ecstasy in which you interact with the inner world, thereby influencing the outer world. Ecstatic trance enables you to participate directly in the work of encountering and transforming your inner structure, which mirrors your reality. Structure determines how energy will flow, where it will be directed, and what new forms and structures will be created. Through the transformation of your inner landscapes, you transform the external landscapes. You create new forms, new structures that are not based on hierarchy, estrangement and exploitation. You renew the Sacred Hoop of life on Earth.

10 ways you can change the world

1. Hold yourself accountable: In its simplest terms, personal accountability is being answerable for your own behavior. Holding yourself accountable is the first step to realizing that you have power over your own life. Accept yourself and your circumstances. Accept responsibility for who you are right now. It is not other people who made you the way you are, but only your own choices, thoughts and actions.

2. Recognize your assumptions: Our perception includes a lot of assumptions which keep us stuck in old patterns. An assumption is usually something we previously learned and do not question. It is part of our belief system. We use our beliefs as assumptions and make inferences, or educated guesses, based on those assumptions. We must do so to make sense of our experiences. Critical thinkers notice the inferences they are making, the assumptions upon which they are basing those inferences, and the point of view they are developing. As people become aware of the inferences they make and the assumptions that underlie those inferences, they begin to take command of their thinking.

3. Cultivate positive thoughts: Your life experiences are the product of habitual beliefs and expectations or, in other words, your appetites. What you ingest or pay attention to becomes what you know as yourself and your world. If you are content with your current situation, that is great. If not, then you must refocus your attention toward more positive thoughts, opinions and attitudes. Shifting your attention into a new pattern will revitalize and renew your life. Pay special attention to the information, ideas and images you allow to enter your mind, for seemingly harmless thought forms shape your experience.

4. Silence your inner critic: Most of us have a voice inside our head, permanently poised to question our competence and destroy our self-esteem. This self-awareness is completely normal. It becomes a problem when that critic takes over and begins running our lives. Sometimes it is so subtle we do not even realize it. To subdue your inner critic, develop the habit of self-reflection. Listen to your thoughts. Acknowledge that your inner critic exists and listen to what it has to say. The negative voice in your head wants to be heard. It needs something, too: a little compassion and assurance. When you give yourself empathy, your confidence will grow and you will step into your power.

5. Know your body: Your body is your compass in the physical world. Both physical and emotional feelings are registered in the body. There is wholeness and grounding in this way of perceiving that is more reliable than the mind. The mind does not really produce any feelings. It chatters incessantly and shows images, but there is no true feeling in it. You feel the truth in your body. Listen to your body's messages. It can guide you toward creating sustainable and lasting change.

6. Learn how to deal with dissonance: Dissonance is the opposite of consonance and means lack of harmony. Earth changes occur when

imbalances need to be corrected. As a species, we have created a great deal of dissonant energy. Negativity, in the form of individual thought patterns multiplied many billions of times, results in widespread strife and calamity. Individual and collective thought forms of conquest, manipulation and oppression are among the most destructive. The best way to deal with this dissonant energy is to move into your heart—into the stillness at your center. You can then hold steady within yourself and not be swept along by external influences. Your inner calm and stability helps to resolve the dissonance and restore consonance.

7. Appropriate destruction: From a shamanic perspective, all creation is based on some form of destruction. In order to create something new, something old first must be destroyed. The old form is taken apart and from its energetic source, something new arises. One powerful universal shamanic motif is the dismemberment of the apprentice during the initiation as a shaman. The individual dies a symbolic death and is then restored and brought back to life. An appropriate destruction measure for anyone would be to get rid of anything that does not contribute to personal growth and learning. This would include the elimination of unnecessary possessions, ideas, habits and limiting beliefs that no longer serve you. Situations, careers or relationships that no longer resonate with you will eventually fall away from your life. When you clear out the old, you make way for the new.

8. Choose to see through your fear: Your fears distort your reality. Fear lulls us into inaction. All the so-called problems in the world are fed by the energy of fear. When you get caught in fear, you end up feeding the negative drama that is playing out on Earth. So each time fear arises, remember to focus on what is happening in the present moment, not what you imagine might happen.

9. Keep your heart space open: One of the most crucial things you can do today is to keep your heart space wide open. In order to keep your heart open, you must be willing to accept what life offers you. If there are challenges on your path, trust that there is a lesson to be learned and growth will occur as a result. We are always tested by the spirits from time to time to see if we have a clear and open heart. You must show the spirit world that you have passion and heart. You must be willing to take risks. It never really ends. You must prove yourself again and again. A meaningful path must have heart.

10. Know that you create your own reality: A fundamental principle of physics is that the observer creates the reality. As an observer, you are personally involved with the creation of your own reality. You are creating your own reality all the time. Every thought you think, every emotion you feel is creating your reality. Give yourself the permission to create the life you want. As responsible human beings, let us affirm a world of peace, harmony and balance. Let us cultivate care for life and one another. See things as they are, in process of change, without fixation on imbalance; see the potential and call it forth.

Appendix A

The Sacred Pipe

According to Lakota legend, the first pipe was brought to Earth 19 generations ago by a divine messenger known as White Buffalo Calf Woman (known in the Lakota language as Pte-san Win-yan). The pipe was given to the people who would not forget—the Oceti Sakowin, or Seven Council Fires of the Lakota, Dakota and Nakota nations. The Buffalo Calf Woman came to the tribes when there was a great famine and instructed them about living in balance with nature. She gifted the people with a sacred bundle containing the White Buffalo Calf Pipe, which still exists to this day and is kept by Chief Arvol Looking Horse of the Cheyenne River Sioux Tribe. Other members of the tribes are also pipe carriers: stewards entrusted with the care of particular ceremonial and personal pipes.

White Buffalo Calf Woman taught them all the things they needed to know about making, handling and caring for the pipe, and about how to use it for praying. She explained to the people that the pipe was a symbol of everything in the world. She told them that the red stone bowl of the pipe represented the Earth Mother and the feminine aspects of the world. The buffalo calf carved in the stone represented all the four-legged animals which live upon the Mother. She told them that the wooden pipe stem represented the Sky Father, the plants and the masculine aspects of the world.

The Buffalo Calf Woman explained that when the stem and bowl were joined, they symbolized a union and a balance between the sacred masculine and the sacred feminine. She told them that the smoking of the pipe linked the smoker to all things in the universe. The smoke from the pipe carried the prayers of the people directly to the Creator. When the pipe was used properly, the buffalo would return and the people would be able to eat well.

Over a period of four days, White Buffalo Calf Woman instructed the people in the Seven Sacred Rites: the seven traditional rituals that use the sacred pipe. When the teaching of the sacred rites was complete, she told the people that she must return to the spirit world. She asked them to honor the teachings of the pipe and to keep it in a sacred manner. Before leaving, the woman told them that within her were four ages, and that she would look upon the people in each age, returning at the end of the fourth age to restore harmony and balance to a troubled world. She said she would send a sign that her return was near in the form of an unusual buffalo, which would be born white.

The holy woman then took leave of the people. As she walked away, she stopped and rolled over four times, changing appearance each time. The first time, she turned into a black buffalo calf; the second time into a red one; the third time into a yellow buckskin one; and finally, the fourth time she rolled over, she turned into a white buffalo calf. These four colors then became associated with the powers of the four directions for the Lakota. The holy entity then disappeared over the horizon. It is said after that day the people honored their pipe, and the buffalo were plentiful.

The prophecy of the White Buffalo Calf Woman

Since then, the vast herds of bison that once migrated across the North American plains have dwindled, hunted into near extinction by nineteenth-century non-indigenous hunters. With their numbers reduced at one time to a mere 500 animals, and the chances of a white calf being born estimated at one in ten million, the fulfillment of the prophecy of White Buffalo Calf Woman seemed improbable. However, a white buffalo calf was born in 1994, and since then at least four to six of these sacred buffalo calves have been born every year. Even more significant was the virgin birth of a white buffalo calf at the Woodland Zoo in Farmington, Pennsylvania in 2006. It would be hard to believe, but Chief Arvol Looking Horse, 19th generation keeper of the White Buffalo Calf Pipe Bundle, has confirmed that a female buffalo gave birth in captivity without artificial insemination or a male buffalo present.[1] Chief Looking Horse believes that these are all signs that the prophecy of the White Buffalo Calf Woman is now coming true.

The prophecy of the White Buffalo Calf Woman is of great spiritual significance to the Lakota and many other tribes. Lakota holy man John Fire Lame Deer once said, "A white buffalo is the most sacred living thing you could ever encounter."[2] Lakota people see the birth of a white buffalo calf as the most significant of prophetic signs. Some Lakota equate the birth of a white buffalo calf to the second coming of Christ. As Oglala Lakota medicine man Floyd Looks For Buffalo Hand puts it, "The arrival of the white buffalo is like the second coming of Christ. It will bring about purity of mind, body, and spirit and unify all nations—black, red, yellow, and white."[3]

When Jesuit priests established missions among the Lakota in 1886, their stories of the Virgin Mary and Jesus became associated with the myth of White Buffalo Calf Woman. The Buffalo Calf Woman's gift of the sacred pipe to the people was likened, by some Lakota, to Mary's gift of Jesus to the people. The syncretic practice of identifying Mary with White Buffalo Calf Woman and Jesus with the sacred pipe continues to this day among Lakota Christians. Lakota and Christian spirituality blend throughout the story of White Buffalo Calf Woman. Even her promise to return to the people mirrors that of Christ. In his book, *Land of the Spotted Eagle*, Oglala Lakota chief Luther Standing Bear referred to White Buffalo Calf Woman as the "Holy Woman" who delivered a version of the Ten Commandments.[4] These Christian influences on the myth are part of the history of change within the story. The story evolves and shapes itself to the people; it grows and adapts to an ever-changing world.

The Sacred Horse Pipe

Along with the birth of sacred white buffalo calves, five spirit horses are heralding the return of the White Buffalo Calf Woman. In 2014, five horses came out of a hand-carved horse effigy pipe that "woke" itself up. A wild and powerful black horse was the first to emerge from the red pipestone horse head pipe bowl. A few weeks later, a white horse with blue eyes came out, followed by a yellow buckskin horse, and then a red horse. These four horses are said to represent the powers of the four directions, and their job is to carry the burden of the people. The fifth horse to arise from the stone bowl of the pipe was a little red sorrel horse. The little red horse is the pipe itself, and is said to be the capstone of all the horses. The little red horse's innocence is what gives him his unique power. In his heart is the light of innocence and purity. Anything evil cannot withstand this divine power and strength.

The Horse Pipe is unique in that it has no (male) wooden stem, it has never been smoked, and it has four keepers/carriers entrusted with its care. It is very powerful, highly focused, and works all the time on behalf of the people. Moreover, this pipe awakened itself, and that has never happened before. Normally, the spirit of a pipe is asleep until it is ritually blessed and awakened through a special ceremony. This pipe awoke with the black horse emerging from it during a time of need. This need has not ceased; in fact this need has grown. Because there is such great need, the Creator gifted the Horse Pipe and its horses to the people. There is more than one of these spirit pipes on the Earth. Since the first horses emerged four years ago, there are now many herds of spirit horses—thousands of them. Their power is unmatched because they come directly from the Creator.

The spirit horses are leading the charge against the darkness manifesting in our world today. Earth changes are intensifying now. Great shifts in energy are taking place at this time. The veil between the spiritual and physical worlds is growing thinner and it is starting to get very dangerous. There is a major battle going on in the spirit world between the light and the dark, and it is spilling over into the material world. The dark is making a bid for power. The light is countering every move made by the dark; the light will ultimately prevail.

In this epic battle between the light and the dark, human beings are being used as commodities by the dark. The dark feeds on human energy, or life force, just like a parasite feeds on its host. The darkness needs the light of our souls, for it has no inner light to sustain it. This is why human souls have been held in slavery or servitude on Earth for centuries. Millions of people are now under the power of darkness. The dark uses mind control to enslave its victims. They are manipulated into believing they cannot be free, but human beings have free will. Freedom of choice is our human birthright and gift from the Creator.

We need to pray for these people and make that a new intention in our rituals and invocations. We need to pray for the liberation of all who are under the power of darkness. Pray for the best possible outcome for all souls, living and dead. The Creator is helping all enslaved souls to choose for themselves. In the struggle between good and evil, we are all being called upon to choose which side we are on—the light or the dark. The horses are very patient and willing to give people (even those working in the dark) every opportunity to choose which side they are on. This is not judgment day. It has nothing to do with religion or ideology. This is about human existence, free will, and each of us claiming our sovereignty.

In the dark age of Kali Yuga, evil rises to the surface of the planet to be eliminated from Earth's energy field. The horses, Jesus and the higher powers are removing the source of evil. You can call upon the horses to clear your home or property of any dark or malevolent energy. Just say the prayer: "In the name of Jesus, I need help." When you do, a horse, or horses, will respond immediately. They are very fast and can be in many places at once. The nastier the dark thing or person is, the bigger the horses become. They go after the darkness and take it away. You do not have to be a Christian to benefit from this prayer. You just have to be sincere in your intent when you speak the words and you will see results.

Reclaiming souls

I call upon the horses every day to connect with me when I drum and to assist me in bringing in the light.[5] One of my jobs is to help earthbound souls cross over. An earthbound soul is one who chooses not to cross over to the other side when their physical existence ends. I ask the horses to assist me in helping lost souls return to the light. All earthbound souls recognize the spirit horses and can communicate with them. The horses give the people the confidence to make the choice to cross over.

There are many techniques and ways to perform psychopomp work. I call in the spirits and the lost souls so they can cross over. I work primarily with the drum and the power of a clear intention to help earthbound souls move beyond their worldly attachments and progress towards the light. When you play a drum, the sound can be heard by the spirits throughout all realms of the spirit world. The sound waves create a bridge between the physical and spiritual planes. In the sound world, a tunnel opens through which souls can pass, or our helping spirits come to us. When you stop playing the drum, the bridge disappears.

We are currently in a time of great transition where a growing number of people are being called to fulfill the sacred role of the psychopomp. Some choose to offer their assistance as a hospice worker or a midwife to the dying—those who hold the edge space between human life and the afterlife. Others, like me, have been called to help those who may be trapped in the spirit realms. Many earthbound souls are enslaved against their will by the dark. The horses will liberate all souls, living or dead, who are under the power of darkness. All we have to do is invoke them. As lightworkers, we have everything we need to reclaim the souls of the living and the dead. We have prayer ties, holy water and horses. The holy Horse, with its mystical powers, offers a promise that the dark times will pass. The light will return. Like a phoenix rising from the ashes, the world will be reborn.

THE GREAT SHIFT

Appendix B

Resources

Foundation for Shamanic Studies: a non-profit organization founded by anthropologist Michael Harner. The FSS is dedicated to the preservation, study, and teaching of shamanic knowledge for the welfare of the planet and its inhabitants. They present the world's foremost training programs in core shamanism and shamanic healing at www.shamanism.org/.

Shamanic Circles: a non-profit organization dedicated to fostering global shamanic community through on-line networking and International Shamanic Community Gatherings at www.shamaniccircles.org/.

Shaman Portal: an organization dedicated to providing individual shamans and shamanic communities with forums that foster environmentalism, social balance and healing at www.shamanportal.org/.

Society for Shamanic Practitioners: a non-profit organization whose goal is to support the re-emergence of shamanic wisdom into modern western culture. They provide a forum for sharing ideas about integrating shamanic practice into contemporary society at www.shamansociety.org/.

The Buddhist Society: an organization founded in 1924, with the object to publish and make known the principles of Buddhism and to encourage the study and practice of those principles at: www.thebuddhistsociety.org/.

The Center of Traditional Taoist Studies: a non-profit theological and educational organization dedicated to promoting Taoism throughout the United States and the world. The Center's curriculum includes traditional Taoist philosophy, religious instruction, and meditation at www.tao.org/.

The Daoist Foundation: a non-profit religious and educational organization dedicated to fostering authentic Daoist (Taoist) study and practice and to preserving and transmitting traditional Daoist culture. They provide classes, texts and resources at www.daoistfoundation.org/.

THE GREAT SHIFT

Endnotes

Introduction

1. Christina Pratt, *An Encyclopedia of Shamanism* (The Rosen Publishing Group, 2007), p. xxii.

Chapter 1: The Great Shift

1. David Houle and Tim Rumage, *This Spaceship Earth* (David Houle 2015), p 4.
2. Eduardo Viveiros de Castro, *Cannibal Metaphysics* (Univocal Publishing, 2014) p. 60.
3. Joan Halifax, *Shamanic Voices: A Survey of Visionary Narratives* (Penguin 1991) p 18.
4. Halifax, *Shamanic Voices*, p. 22.

Chapter 2: Navigating the Great Shift

1. Sri Chinmoy, *Fifty Freedom-Boats to One Golden Shore, part 3*, (Agni Press, 1974).
2. Beau Lotto, *Deviate: The Science of Seeing Differently* (Hachette Books, 2017).
3. Lotto, *Deviate: The Science of Seeing Differently*.
4. Learn how to hake your own holy water at: https://www.wikihow.com/Make-Your-Own-Holy-Water.
5. Mihaly Csikszentmihalyi, *Flow: The Psychology of Optimal Experience* (Harper & Row, 1990).
6. Csikszentmihalyi, *Flow: The Psychology of Optimal Experience*.

Chapter 3: Harnessing the Power of Drumming

1. Sule Greg Wilson, *The Drummer's Path* (Destiny Books, 1992), p. XII.
2. Mariko Namba Walter and Eva Jane Neumann Fridman, *Shamanism: An Encyclopedia of World Beliefs, Practices, and Culture* (ABC-CLIO, 2004), p. 95.
3. Robert Lawrence Friedman, *Healing Power of the Drum* (White Cliffs Media, 2000).
4. Michael Winkelman, *Shamanism: The Neural Ecology of Consciousness and Healing* (Bergin & Garvey; 2000), p. 148.
5. Ted Andrews, *Animal Speak: The Spiritual & Magical Powers of Creatures Great & Small* (Llewellyn Publications, 1996), p. 93.
6. You can download this free (EPUB format) eBook on my website at: http://www.shamanicdrumming.com/How-to-Make-Drums.epub
7. Patricia Peterson, "Shuunka Drumming Circle." Hancock Parks. May 2010. Web. 28 June 2018. <http://www.hancockparks.com/TellUsYourStory/May2010Story.aspx>.
8. Michael Drake, *Shamanic Drumming Circles Guide* (Talking Drum Pub., 2014).
9. Ed Mikenas, "Drums, Not Drugs," *Percussive Notes*, Volume 37 #2, 1999.
10. Wallace Black Elk and William S. Lyon, *Black Elk: The Sacred Ways of a Lakota* (Harper & Row, 1990), p. 149.

11. Michael Winkelman, "Complementary Therapy for Addiction: Drumming Out Drugs," *American Journal of Public Health*; Apr 2003, Vol. 93 Issue 4, p 647, 5p.
12. Joseph Rael, Mary Marlow, *Being and Vibration* (Council Oak Books, 1993), p. 163.

Chapter 4: Divining the Way to Harmony

1. Lao Tzu, *Tao Te Ching*, chapter 55.
2. A changing line is a line that changes from yin to yang or the other way around, resulting in a new hexagram related to your query.
3. *Ni Tseh Collection on I Ching Studies* (University of California at Irvine, n.p. 1884).
4. Richard Wilhelm, *The I Ching* (Princeton University Press, 1950) p. liv.
5. Thomas Cleary, *Vitality, Energy, Spirit: A Taoist Sourcebook* (Shambhala, 1991).
6. Melinda Maxfield, *Drumming the I Ching* (Melinda Maxfield, 1989).
7. You can consult the I Ching online at my website: http://ShamanicDrumming.com/iching/index.html.
8. Joseph Needham, *Science and Civilization in China*. 2 vols. (Cambridge University Press, 1954).
9. George Leonard, *The Silent Pulse* (Bantam New Age Books, 1981).
10. Richard Wilhelm, *The I Ching*, p. 139.
11. Lao Tzu, *Tao Te Ching*, chapter 56.
12. Richard Wilhelm, *The I Ching*, p. 297.

Chapter 5: Practicing the Art of Shapeshifting

1. John Perkins, *Shapeshifting: Techniques for Global and Personal Transformation*, (Destiny Books 1997), p. 9.
2. Dorothy H. Eber, "Recording the Spirit World," *Natural History Magazine*, Sept, 2002, p. 54.
3. Don Dream Seeker Fasthorse, personal communication, March 14, 1992.
4. Ted Andrews, *Animal Speak: The Spiritual & Magical Powers of Creatures Great & Small* (Llewellyn Publications, 1996), p. 224.
5. Michael Drake, *Power Animal Drumming*. Talking Drum Publications, 2010. CD.
6. Nicholas Noble Wolf. "Shamanic Drum and Shamanic Drumming." Nicholas Noble Wolf. Web. 9 Sept. 2018. <http://www.nicholasnoblewolf.com/q_and_a/drum_drumming.html>.
7. R. Buckminster Fuller, *Critical Path* (St. Martin's Griffin, 1982).
8. John Perkins, *Shapeshifting*, (Destiny Books, 1997), p. 9.

Chapter 6: Taking the Shamanic Journey

1. Michael J. Harner. "In Memoriam." The Foundation for Shamanic Studies. Web. 06 June 2018. <https://www.shamanism.org/index.php>
2. Kira Van Deusen, *Singing Story, Healing Drum: Shamans and Storytellers of Turkic Siberia* (McGill-Queen's Press, 2005), p. 122.
3. Felicitas D. Goodman, *Jewels on the Path: A Spirit Notebook, vol. II* (Cuyamungue Institute, 1994), p. 55.

4. Kira Van Deusen, "Shamanism and Music in Tuva and Khakassia," *Shaman's Drum*, No. 47, Winter 1997, p. 24.
5. Michael Drake, *Shamanic Journey Drumming*. Talking Drum Publications, 2008. CD.
6. C. Michael Smith, *Jung and Shamanism in Dialogue* (Paulist Press, 1997), p 16.
7. Belinda Gore, *Ecstatic Body Postures: An Alternate Reality Book* (Bear & Company; Workbook edition, 1995), p 192.
8. Susan Mokelke, "Ethical Considerations in Shamanic Healing." *Shamanism*, December 2008, Issue 21.
9. Samudranath, *Cities of Lightning: The Iconography of Thunder-Beings in the Oriental Traditions* (Blue Dolphin, 2000), p. 12.

Chapter 7: Becoming the Hollow Bone

1. Thomas E. Mails, *Fools Crow: Wisdom and Power* (Council Oak Books, 2001), p. 27.
2. Only enrolled members of federally recognized Native American tribes are allowed to possess eagle bone whistles, though replicas are available.
3. Thomas E. Mails, *Fools Crow*, p. 27.
4. Susan Grimaldi, "Tuvan Shamanism Comes to America." *Shamanism*, (1998). Susan Grimaldi. Web. 28 June 2018. <http://www.susangrimaldi.com/docs/tuvamerica.pdf>.
5. Livia Kohn, *The Taoist Experience: An Anthology.* (State University of New York Press, 1993), p. 320.

Chapter 8: Changing the World

1. Gary Zukav. "Intentions and Effects." *HuffPost*. 25 Jan. 2014. Web.13 June 2018. <https://www.huffingtonpost.com/gary-zukav/life-choices_b_4228881.html>
2. Wynne Hanner. "Awakening into Dreamtime: The Shaman's Journey." *Planet Shifter Magazine*. 3 Aug. 2011. Web. 2 May 2018. <http://www.planetshifter.com/node/1912>.
3. Mihaly Csikszentmihalyi, *Flow: The Psychology of Optimal Experience* (Harper & Row, 1990).

Appendix A: The Sacred Pipe

1. Chief Arvol Looking Horse, "Arvol Looking Horse: Letters to the People," Great Spirit Mother. 12 Nov. 2007. Web. 13 July 2018. <http://www.great-spirit-mother.org/_/arvol_looking_horse_letters_to_the_people.htm>.
2. John Lame Deer and Richard Erdoes, *Lame Deer, Seeker of Visions* (Simon and Schuster, 1994).
3. Floyd Looks For Buffalo Hand, "The Legend & Importance of the White Buffalo," Lakota Ranch. Web.12 July 2018. <http://lightningmedicinecloud.com/legend.html>.
4. Luther Standing Bear, *Land of the Spotted Eagle* (University of Nebraska Press, 1978).
5. You can invoke the horses using the "Horse Chant." Listen at https://archive.org/details/SacredSongsAndChants.

About the Author

Michael Drake is an internationally regarded writer and recording artist. He is the author of *The Shamanic Drum: A Guide to Sacred Drumming*, *I Ching: The Tao of Drumming*, *Shamanic Drumming: Calling the Spirits* and *Shamanic Drumming Circles Guide*. His musical albums include *Shamanic Journey Drumming*, *Power Animal Drumming* and *Shaman's Drums*. His articles have appeared in numerous publications, including *Awareness*, *Sacred Hoop* and *Mother Earth News*.

Raised in a conservative Baptist church, Michael had his first ecstatic experience as a youth at a church revival, an evangelistic meeting intended to reawaken interest in religion. This state of rapture and trancelike elation inspired his spiritual quest for meaning and fulfillment. At a crucial point in his search, Michael came in touch with the transforming power of shamanic drumming and discovered his true calling. Inspired by his research and experiences, Michael founded Talking Drum Publications in 1991 in order to share the healing power of rhythm with the global drumming community. For the past twenty-five years he has been facilitating drum circles and workshops nationwide. To learn more, visit Michael's website at http://ShamanicDrumming.com.

www.ingramcontent.com/pod-product-compliance
Lightning Source LLC
Chambersburg PA
CBHW060315050426
42448CB00009B/1846